Poverty
and
Social
Exclusion
in Wales

D1335764

The Bevan Foundation

About the Bevan Foundation

The Bevan Foundation supports social justice in Wales through research, discussion
and publications. Our work helps to set and inform the public policy agenda in Wales,
particularly on poverty and social exclusion.

We are independent of government, political parties or interest groups. Membership is
open to individuals, third sector organizations, businesses and government bodies.

The Bevan Foundation
Innovation Centre
Festival Drive
Ebbw Vale
Blaenau Gwent
NP23 8XA

Tel: 01495 356702   info@bevanfoundation.org   www.bevanfoundation.org

Registered Charity No. 1104191

ISBN 978-1-904767-44-2

Published in December 2010. © 2010

The contents and opinions expressed in this paper are those of the authors only.

Acknowledgments

The Bevan Foundation gratefully acknowledges the financial support of the European
Year 2010 for Combating Poverty and Social Exclusion from the European Union and
Department for Work and Pensions.

Contents

Foreword

1. Overview of Poverty and Social Exclusion

Tackling poverty and social exclusion   1
Huw Lewis AM

Income and wealth in Wales   7
Peter Kenway

2. Aspects of Poverty

Child poverty in Wales: Where there's the will, is there a way?   29
Sean O'Neill

Amy's story   42

Work, worklessness and poverty amongst adults in Wales   45
Victoria Winckler

Jane's story   53

Sian's story   56

Older people and poverty in Wales   59
Graeme Francis

Margaret's story   70

3. Education

Educational equity and school performance in Wales   73
David Egan

Mark's story   88

The Loners' Club   91
Mark Atkinson

4. Housing

Raising the roof? Housing, poverty and social exclusion   93
Tamsin Stirling

James's story   102

5. Health

Thinking upstream the challenge of health inequalities in Wales   105
Michael Shepherd

Ida's story   120

Naomi's story   124

6. Material poverty and Social Exclusion

Financial exclusion   127
Lindsey Kearton

Fuel poverty in Wales   133
James Radcliffe

The downside of the great car economy: transport poverty in Wales   141
Lee Waters

Digital exclusion, divided Wales   147
Victoria Winckler and James Radcliffe

7. Conclusion

Headlines and "small things": filling in the picture of poverty and   155
social exclusion
Gideon Calder

Annex. CONFERENCE REPORT

Morning Session   161
    Keynote Speakers
    Workshops

Afternoon Session   170
    Two Sisters – a film
    Knowledge café

    Beverley Humphreys in conversation with Mark Atkinson   173
    and Dilys Price

FOREWORD

WHEN 2010 WAS FORMALLY DECLARED the European Year for Combating Poverty and Social Exclusion in 2008, few people would have anticipated that the progress made towards eradicating poverty in Wales over the last decade was about to go into reverse. Up until declaration year, child and pensioner poverty were in steady decline and, although working-age poverty was proving more stubborn, employment was nevertheless up and unemployment down compared with the start of the decade. But by 2010, unemployment had soared to levels not seen for ten years, child poverty was increasing again and progress towards eradicating working-age and older people's poverty had effectively stalled. Once again, hundreds of thousands of people in Wales are living below the poverty threshold.

The aim of the European Year for Combating Poverty and Social Exclusion is to give voice to the concerns of people who have to live with poverty and social exclusion, and to challenge stereotypes about poverty. Across the European Union, all kinds of organisations have been working on these themes. The Bevan Foundation, a charity which promotes social justice in Wales through research, discussion and publications, was delighted to deliver the year's 'regional activity' in Wales. Our activities aimed to explore the root causes of poverty and social exclusion in Wales, listen to the experiences of people living in poverty and question perceptions about them.

In choosing our EY2010 activities in Wales we were mindful that although 2010 would soon be over, poverty and social exclusion persist. We therefore wanted our work for EY2010 to leave a legacy. Some of the legacy would be tangible outputs, like this book, that would be used into 2011 and hopefully beyond, but we also wanted help to shape public policy on and perceptions of poverty.

So what did we do? First, we organised a conference which was held on 23rd September 2010, involving more than 80 people. A report of the conference is in the Annex to this book.

Then, we commissioned a video about living in poverty and building routes out, entitled 'Two Sisters', which is available on http://www.youtube.com/user/enginehouseprod. The powerful portrayal of Gemma and Donna Griffiths' lives has proved immensely popular, attracting considerable interest from the Welsh media and public alike, being screened on the Community channel shortly.

We have also prepared a website to bring together information about poverty and social exclusion in Wales and provide links to other sources of information and action, at www.ey2010.bevanfoundation.org. We hope the website will be a resource for all those concerned about poverty and social exclusion in Wales.

Last, but by no means least, we have published this book. We hope it provides an opportunity to analyse and reflect on poverty and social exclusion in Wales and contributes to the policy agenda for the coming decade. It has a broad range of contributions, covering poverty amongst different age groups as well as different aspects of social exclusion, and also includes 'stories' about individuals' experiences. It is published, coincidentally, thirty years after a seminal book, Gareth Rees and Teresa Rees's *Poverty and Social Inequality in Wales*[1]. Whilst the ensuing chapters show that people's lives are still marred by poverty and social exclusion then as now, in many ways the causes of poverty and people's experiences of it have changed significantly since 1980.

We are very grateful to the many organisations and individuals who have helped to make our EY2010 activities a success and who have helped with the publication of this book. They are too numerous to mention individually, but the activities would not have happened without the input of the staff and students of Merthyr Tydfil College, the speakers and panellists at the conference, and the authors of the chapters and stories in this book. We are also grateful to all the behind-the-scenes workers who make these things happen.

We also gratefully acknowledge the contribution of the European Union and Department of Work and Pensions EY2010 grant, without which these activities would not have been possible.

Victoria Winckler
Bevan Foundation

Notes   *1* Rees, G. and Rees, T.L., eds. (1980) *Poverty and Social Inequality in Wales*. London: Croom Helm

1.

OVERVIEW
of
Poverty
and
Social
Exclusion

Tackling
poverty
and social exclusion*

Huw Lewis AM

THERE CAN BE NO MORE important social issue than the fight against poverty and social exclusion which blights the lives and life chances of so many of our citizens in Wales. That is why tackling poverty remains a fundamental aim of the Welsh Assembly Government.

I am pleased that, in Wales, the Bevan Foundation successfully bid for funding under the European Year for Combating Poverty to run awareness-raising activities. The Bevan Foundation has a proud record of its work in this area of policy and I'm delighted to be able to support the Foundation as much as possible.

The activities in connection with the Year are allowing us to raise the profile of the work across Wales to tackle poverty and improve the life chances of some of our most disadvantaged people.

I would like to talk to you about what we, in the Welsh Assembly Government, are doing to tackle the difficult issues of poverty and social exclusion amongst some of our most disadvantaged groups.

Given my specific Ministerial responsibility for co-ordinating our action on child poverty, I would also like to talk to you about what the Welsh Assembly Government is doing in order to support the UK Child Poverty Act target to eradicate child poverty by 2020.

Poverty in Wales

Before we look at the Assembly Government's policy response to tackling poverty I think it's always helpful to look at the situation in Wales and the hard facts.

The official measure of poverty is the proportion of households who have an income which is less than 60 per cent of the median income. By way of example, for a couple with two children aged 5 and 14 this equates to a weekly income of £333 per week or below, after housing costs have been deducted.

Over the past ten years in Wales, overall poverty has fallen by three percentage points, compared with two percentage points for the UK as a whole. However, the extent of poverty for all groups in Wales (apart from older people) is slightly higher than for the UK as a whole.

Looking at the position of certain groups:

* Speech delivered on 23rd September 2010

- For working-age adults – after housing costs have been taken into account 22 percent are living below the poverty threshold in Wales. This is the same as ten years ago whilst for the UK as a whole it has gone up by one percentage point.

- For children – 32 percent are living in poverty. This has fallen by four percentage points in Wales over the last ten years whilst for the UK it has fallen by two percentage points.

- And for older people – 18 per cent are living below the poverty line. This has fallen by eight percentage points over the past ten years whilst for the UK as a whole it has fallen by ten percentage points.

Key policies and programmes for tackling poverty

These are just the stark facts and figures but I want to make it absolutely clear that the continued existence of poverty in a modern, civilised and progressive country such as Wales is unacceptable to the Welsh Assembly Government. And the current economic climate makes it even more important that we remain committed in the Assembly Government to prioritising the needs of the poorest and protecting the most vulnerable.

"the continued existence of poverty in a modern, civilised and progressive country such as Wales is unacceptable

Those living in poverty are vulnerable in a number of different ways. We know that they are more at risk of poor health and poor educational attainment, have lower skills and aspirations, and are more likely to be low paid, unemployed and welfare dependent.

We already have an array of polices and programmes across the Assembly Government which are aimed at reducing poverty. If I may I would like to mention just a few here – to demonstrate the Assembly Government's absolute commitment to tackling both the causes and the effects of poverty.

In terms of reducing poverty levels we know that being in well paid work is the most sustainable way out of poverty. As well as working with the UK Government to support employability we have also developed a range of 'made in Wales' policies which will complement these efforts.

Skills that Work for Wales is the Assembly Government's skills and employment strategy which responds to the acknowledged need to raise the level of skills in Wales. And for those who are made redundant, we have the *ReAct* programme which provides additional financial support for retraining to those who have lost their jobs. These are just two examples of how the Assembly Government has moved swiftly to mitigate the effects of the current economic climate.

Wales also has a very high number of people who are not engaged with the labour market at all and are classified as being economically inactive for reasons of ill-health or because of family or caring duties. We have a number of programmes in place to support labour market engagement but two programmes – *Want 2 Work[1]* and *Genesis 2[2]* – are specifically designed to work with people on sickness benefit or with lone parents who have become completely disconnected from the labour market.

In addition to reducing worklessness, boosting family income is vital. Wales's first Financial Inclusion Strategy '*Taking Everyone into Account*' was published in July last year.

Concentrations of poverty are the cause of entrenched social problems and those living in our poorest areas face multiple challenges. We believe that in order to address issues holistically and with the aim of achieving sustainable change, it is appropriate that part of our response to tackling child poverty is through our *Communities First* programme. This initiative remains fundamental to our vision of building a better Wales, including for those living in the most disadvantaged areas.

> **Concentrations of poverty are the cause of entrenched social problems**

The Welsh Assembly Government acknowledges the problem of poverty among older people. Within our devolved powers and through our *Strategy for Older People in Wales* we have continued to develop and implement a range of policies and programmes to combat the poverty that is faced by older people.

In a number of local authorities there has been a tremendous effort to increase benefit take-up by older people. Rhondda Cynon Taf and Caerphilly have both implemented different but successful schemes to maximise benefit take up in their areas. In Rhondda Cynon Taf a dedicated team was set up through the council's older people strategy unit that will visit older people and complete a benefit check and any relevant forms. In Caerphilly the 50+ Positive Action Partnership has arranged for partners already offering advice on benefits to meet up and explore new ways of joint working. These two schemes have assisted older people in claiming around £20m extra in benefits. All local authorities have established Older People's Forums to promote the engagement and participation of older people in decisions that effect them.

Pensions and benefits policies are the responsibility of the UK Government but we have worked with them in initiatives such Link-Age Wales to maximise the take up of pensions and benefits. We have also worked closely with Local Government in Wales to encourage the take-up of council tax and housing benefits by older people.

Socially Excluded Groups

The Welsh Assembly Government is also aware that there are a number of other socially excluded groups who are particularly at risk of poverty. To help address this we have developed a number of policies, including the *Refugee Inclusion Strategy* which aims to support and enable refugees to rebuild their lives in Wales and make a full contribution to Welsh society.

We have also developed a policy framework that will have important implications for the provision of services for Gypsies and Travellers in Wales. This new policy framework has culminated in the first Gypsy and Traveller Strategy which will be launched early in 2011.

Disability also presents a significant risk factor for poverty and we in the Assembly Government have a number of polices and programmes in place to support families coping with disability – for example, an extra £500,000 available over two years to raise awareness and increase uptake of the benefits available to parents and carers of children with disabilities.

Child poverty

Given my Ministerial lead for child poverty, I would like to spend a little time talking to you about the work being done in this area. In December last year, I was very pleased to accept the role of Deputy Minister for Children with special responsibility for co-ordinating our action to reduce child poverty in Wales.

> **we do not have all the answers to tackle the multi-faceted nature of child poverty**

The Welsh Assembly Government is aware that we do not have all the answers to tackle the multi-faceted nature of child poverty. In 2008 we therefore established a Child Poverty Expert Group which fulfils a 'One Wales' commitment to set up a group of experts in the field of child poverty who now provide us with advice and guidance on the policy response we need to have in place to reduce child poverty in Wales.

This work has taken a major step forward with the launch of our new *Child Poverty Strategy and Delivery Plan* which sets the strategic direction for action in Wales to eradicate child poverty. The Strategy issued in May for a three month consultation period which ended on 12th August.

I am pleased to report that in excess of 160 consultation responses have been received, and over the next few months, the Child Poverty Unit will be working closely with policy colleagues from across the Welsh Assembly Government with the view to publishing a revised Strategy and Delivery Plan later this year and, importantly, driving the strategy forward.

We know, of course, that many of the tools to reduce child poverty levels, for instance control of the tax and benefits system, are in the hands of the UK Government. Some may, therefore, argue that reducing the levels of poverty that so damages the lives of families across the UK is primarily a UK Government responsibility. I do not accept that. Now is the very worst time to tuck tail and run!

That is why we moved quickly to use our new legislative powers to introduce new legislation to underpin our efforts to reduce child poverty in Wales. I am very proud that the Children and Families (Wales) Measure, which received Privy Council approval on the 10th February 2010, made us the first of the four governments in the UK to place a statutory duty on public bodies to tackle child poverty.

Our new Measure placed upon us a legal duty to develop our new Child Poverty Strategy for Wales, but, crucially, similar duties will also be placed on local government, which provides education and social care, and our health service, as well as our main cultural and sports bodies.

Our new Child Poverty Strategy sets a new direction for developing more effective local delivery arrangements to meet the needs of low income families.

We know that families in poverty face a huge range of difficult issues, including unemployment, education, health, housing, parenting, benefits, debt, skills, and substance misuse. As part of our new Child Poverty Strategy we will be developing a new approach to providing support to families living in poverty – at the local level. This approach is already being tried in several local authority areas, and is showing great promise in bringing multiple agencies together to work with families on a holistic basis.

But even the best approaches aren't delivering for families in a fully integrated way yet, for example by addressing the income and work issues needed to tackle poverty in the round. That is why in July I launched our *Families First Pioneers* initiative. I have asked two consortia of local authorities, one in North Wales and one in South Wales, to develop integrated, preventative and, where they can, innovative approaches to lifting families out of poverty.

Families First is about placing the family at the centre of our anti-poverty work, especially those families who need the most support. I want that support to be continuous, not episodic as it has been so often in the past, but continuous in an empowering way, so that families, with our help, can eventually lift themselves out of poverty. I have asked the two consortia to develop a model which will show how they will take this work forward. When they do that, we will have a better idea of how we will help deliver services to families in a better, more efficient and more integrated way.

These are just some of the things that the Welsh Assembly Government is doing to help combat poverty and social exclusion in Wales. Offering all our children a decent start in life, ensuring that no child is held back because of economic disadvantage or poverty of aspiration – these are basic but vital values that separate the good society from the bad.

Whatever constraints prevent us from transforming our country to the extent that we would like now, it is nothing less than our duty to provide the next generation with the tools and the foundations to be able to make that change in the future. You simply cannot do that when nearly a third of children in Wales are growing up in poverty.

The UK Government is using 'deficit reduction' as cover for the greatest assault on state intervention in a generation. If we are to be true to our

" it is nothing less than our duty to provide the next generation with the tools and the foundations to be able to make that change in the future

values here in Wales – we must steer a very different course. Soon the Welsh public realm will differ starkly from that over the border. Our continuing commitment to children in poverty will be just one such difference.

Huw Lewis
is Deputy Minister
for Children,
Welsh Assembly
Government

Notes   1 A scheme to help people who are economically inactive to find work
       2 A project to address barriers to work such as lack of childcare support, transport accessibility, debt, alcohol and drug misuse, and work-limiting health conditions

Income
and wealth
in Wales

Peter Kenway

MR BLAIR'S PLEDGE IN 1999 that child poverty would be ended within a generation revived an idea that had been long suppressed. At the same time, though, it confined its revival to the narrowest of channels. That idea was that some aspects at least of the distribution of income and wealth have social as well as private consequences. As a result, they are properly matters of governmental concern.

The background to this break in thinking from the previous Conservative government – a break, it should be noted, which did not take place until 18 months into the life of the government elected in 1997 – was the steep rise in income inequality during the 18 years of Conservative government. As the table shows, compared with the last three full years of the 1970s Labour government, income inequality rose in both the lower and upper halves of the income distribution as well as overall. By contrast, over the 15 years prior to Mrs Thatcher's election in 1979, income inequality had come down slightly, especially in the lower half of the distribution.

Table 1: Income inequality measures prior to three political turning points: Great Britain

	50:10 ratio	90:50 ratio	Gini coefficient
1961-1963	1.90	1.73	0.27
1976-1978	1.76	1.72	0.25
1994/95-1996/97	2.33	2.13	0.37

Interpretation. The 50:10 ratio measures the ratio of income at the 50th percentile (the median) to the income at the 10th percentile (that is, 10% of the way up from the bottom of the income distribution). The 90:50 ratio measures the ratio of income at the 90th percentile (10% of the way down from the top of the income distribution) to median income. In both cases, the larger the statistic, the greater the degree of income inequality.

Up to a point, the two are measures of 'lower half' and 'upper half' income inequality respectively – although only 'up to point' given the incomes of the more than 5 million people below the 10th percentile and 5 million above the 90th do not enter in. By contrast, the Gini coefficient is a complete measure of income inequality (i.e. very low and very high incomes count here), lying between zero (perfect income equality) and one (perfect income inequality, that is, one person has everything).

Source: Family Expenditure Survey and Family Resources survey via Institute for Fiscal Studies, 2010, IFSOnlinespreadsheet (inequality). Statistics are on the after housing costs (AHC) basis.

At the same time, however, the emergence of this subject as a concern of governments was strictly limited. First and foremost, it was restricted to a concern about child poverty which in practice means the incomes of families with dependent children. Second, by measuring poverty in relation to median income, it restricted itself to what was going on in the lower half of the income distribution only.[1] Third, by setting its targets in relation to the proportions below a particular low income threshold, it restricted its concern to the scale, or extent, of poverty rather than its depth.

One further restriction was also important. This was the belief that the route out of poverty inevitably involved paid work. As a prescription for achieving an income above the poverty threshold, this was problematic even in the late 1990's. What it did, however, was to marry the concern with poverty per se with the idea that being brought up in a workless household was a bad thing for a child irrespective of whether income was above or below some particular threshold.

Scope of the chapter

As the main poles of the previous UK government's concerns in this area, child poverty and children living in workless households define the terms of the public debate on this subject for the best part of a decade. Any account of income and wealth in Wales is therefore wise to begin here since this is the terrain that is most familiar. The first section of this chapter therefore reviews the progress of these two key indicators; along with a small selection of supporting ones, in a manner that could have (and has) been done at any point the early 2000s.

For so long as it is an account of 'progress', a narrow focus on a few chosen statistics is sufficient if hardly insightful. Once progress ceases, however, the thinness of this approach provides few clues as to why things have turned sour. Rather than dig deeper in the familiar terrain, the rest of the chapter takes a wider view, using for inspiration a chapter (of the same name) written 30 years ago.[2] The second section of the chapter looks at the Welsh economy (and the economist's measure of income known as 'gross value added' or GVA), as well as earnings in Wales (to which GVA is related). The third then looks in more detail at household incomes in Wales, including a brief view of household wealth. The aim of this is to present a picture of where Wales now stands, both in relation to both its own past and other parts of the UK. As a rule, comparisons with other parts of the UK are restricted to Northern Ireland, Scotland and the English North East (as usually the poorest of the nine English regions). Figures for England and the UK as a whole are also given for completeness. The final section of the chapter draws conclusions.

The ten year record on child poverty and worklessness
The measurement and definition of poverty

Despite having been a priority for so long, data on child poverty both across the UK in general and in Wales in particular is of poor quality, being produced annually a full year or more after the period to which it applies has ended. Worse still, official statisticians only report figures for Wales and the English regions as three-year averages. Given the wild swings in the annual numbers for Wales, such caution is amply justified – but it does have serious political consequences.[3]

Given these constraints, statistics on poverty are reported here for three periods of time, namely: (i) the average for the latest three years 2006/07 to 2008/09; (ii) the average for ten years earlier, that is 1996/97 to 1998/99, which can be thought of as the situation prevailing just prior to the formation of the first Welsh Assembly Government; and (iii) the average for the three years 2003/04 to 2005/06. The significance of this point will become clear in a moment.

A household is counted as having a 'low income' ('poverty' for short) if its income is less than 60 per cent of the median UK household income for the year in question. The value of this 60 per cent threshold in terms of pounds per week varies according to how many adults and children live in the household. For example, in 2008/09 it was worth £119 for a single adult with no dependent children, £247 for a lone parent with two children aged 5 and 14, £206 for a couple with no dependent children and £333 for a couple with children aged 5 and 14. These sums of money are measured after deduction of income tax, council tax and housing costs (including rents, mortgage interest, buildings insurance and water charges).[4] They represent what the household has available to spend on everything else it needs, from food and heating to travel and entertainment.

Calculated in relation to average income, this measure is self-evidently relative. But that does not mean that it is only some lesser problem called 'relative poverty' that is being measured. Rather, it reflects the view that poverty is inherently relative, when someone is so short of resources that they are unable to attain the minimum norms for the society in which they live. This was as much the concept of poverty used by the 18th century economist and moral philosopher Adam Smith as it was of Professor Peter Townsend who re-founded poverty studies in Britain in the 1960s. Whether it is sufficient to measure poverty in relation to income at a point in time is a reasonable question. The use of both direct measures of material deprivation, income measured over a longer period of time, and income in relation to fixed thresholds, are sensible supplementary measures. But debates around measurement should not be confused with debates around what it means.

> **debates around measurement of poverty should not be confused with debates around what it means**

Child poverty in Wales

Table 2 shows the proportion of children in poverty in Wales and the selected other regions and countries of the UK for the latest three year period, the corresponding period ten years earlier, and the period 2003/04 to 2005/06. The story here for Wales is very clear: at 32 per cent, child poverty in Wales is some four percentage points down on where it was ten years earlier – a fall of one ninth – but is up by some two percentage points on where it was in the middle years of the 21st century's first decade.[5] In bottoming like this around 2004/05, Wales was not at all alone since this was the pattern across the UK as a whole as well as the English regions. In terms of the number of children involved, 32 per cent represents some 195,000 children, a fall of some 40,000 on the number in poverty ten years earlier.

Table 2: The proportion of children in low income households

	1996/97 to 1998/99	2003/04 to 2005/06	2006/07 to 2008/09
Wales	36%	28%	32%
Northern Ireland		27%	26%
Scotland	32%	25%	25%
England	34%	29%	31%
- of which: North East	40%	32%	34%
UK	34%	29%	31%

Source: Department for Work and Pensions, 2010, Households Below Average Income, table 4.13ts. Data for Northern Ireland not available before 2002/03.

> **The falls recorded... were unprecedented and deserve to be seen as almost a golden period.**

One way of summing this up is to say that across England and Wales, the rise in child poverty over the three years since about 2004/05 is equal to about half of the fall in child poverty over the previous seven. In broad terms, the governments' aim for that first period was a fall in child pverty of a quarter. Although this was not achieved anywhere, Wales and Scotland came close, falling short (by a per cent or two at most) that should not be regarded as significant. The falls recorded at that time were unprecedented and deserve to be seen as almost a golden period.

A couple of other points on this table. First, the child poverty rate in Wales was throughout the period a little lower than that in the English North East (which itself was lower than the rate in London). Second, over the period Wales moved closer to the UK average. This latter reflects a wider pattern in which the recorded falls in child poverty rates over the ten year period were around twice as great across the English North and South West, Wales and Scotland as they were over the English South East and Midlands.

The measurement and definition of poverty

A big part of the explanation for the greater fall in child poverty across the north and west of the British Isles is that the proportion of children in workless families also fell further in these regions (Table 3). Over the nine years from 1999 to 2008, while the proportion of children in workless households fell by only two percentage points across England as a whole, it fell by three in Scotland, more than five in Wales and the English North East and nearly seven in Northern Ireland. With three quarters of children in workless households being in poverty – more than twice the overall rate – disproportionate falls in worklessness will translate into disproportionate falls in child poverty.

Table 3: The proportion of children in workless households

	1999 Q2	*2005 Q2*	*2008 Q2*	*2009 Q2*
Wales	21%	17%	16%	20%
Northern Ireland	20%	16%	13%	18%
Scotland	18%	16%	15%	16%
England	18%	16%	16%	17%
- of which: North East	25%	19%	20%	21%

Source: Office for National Statistics, 2010, Labour Force Survey.

Although most of the fall in worklessness between 1999 and 2008 had taken place by 2005, there is no sign of any rise up till 2008: indeed in Wales, the proportion fell by a further one percentage point over the three year period. What this hints at is that the rise in child poverty after 2005 was not likely to have been caused by rising worklessness, something which the poverty statistics themselves confirm. Since reliable statistics on the child poverty according to work status are simply not available for Wales, the UK-wide story will have to suffice. Here, after falling from a peak of 2.1 million in 1998/99 to 1.7 million in 2003/04, the number of children belonging to working families in poverty had risen to 2 million by 2005/06 and 2.2 million a year later.[6] As a share of all the children in poverty, this represents 56 per cent. If for no other reason than that it contradicts the simple idea that work is the route out of poverty, in-work poverty must be treated very seriously. Any theory or policy about how to reduce child poverty that does not give in-work poverty its due attention cannot any longer expect to be taken seriously.

> **in-work poverty must be treated very seriously**

The final column of Table 3 shows that there can also be no grounds for complacency on out-of-work poverty in Wales. Having held steady through to 2008, by the second quarter of 2009, the proportion of children in workless households in Wales had risen in a year by four percentage points, eroding almost all of what had been gained in the previous nine years.

Pensioner poverty in Wales

If the fall in child poverty has disappointed, the fall in pensioner poverty has exceeded expectations. Although the fall of a third in pensioner poverty in Wales is rather less than the UK average, this may just reflect a lower starting point, Wales's 18 per cent figure for the latest three years being identical to the UK and England averages. Pensioner poverty is lower in Scotland and higher in Northern Ireland.

Table 4: The proportion of pensioners in low income households

	1996/97 to 1998/99	2003/04 to 2005/06	2006/07 to 2008/09
Wales	26%	20%	18%
Northern Ireland		19%	22%
Scotland	29%	18%	14%
England	29%	18%	18%
- of which: North East	32%	17%	18%
UK	29%	18%	18%

Source: Department for Work and Pensions, 2010, Households Below Average Income, table 6.8ts. Data for Northern Ireland not available before 2002/03.

The 18 per cent figure corresponds to some 110,000 pensioners in poverty, a fall of some 40,000 on ten years earlier.

Taken together with the fall in the number of children in poverty, the net effect has been to alter the balance of poverty in Wales among the three age groups, namely children, pensioners and working-age. Ten years ago, the 235,000 children and 145,000 pensioners in poverty accounted for almost exactly half of all the people in poverty in Wales. Ten years later, the falls in the numbers in these two groups, alongside a negligible change in the number of working-age in poverty – some 370,000 – means that working age people now constitute a clear majority of those in poverty (around 55 per cent). Just as in-work poverty contradicts simple ideas about work being the route out, the extent of working-age poverty shows the incompleteness of anti-poverty strategies that focus explicitly on children and implicitly on pensioners.

The Welsh economy, population, productivity and earnings
The size of the Welsh economy

Gross Value Added' (GVA) is the national statistician's way of measuring the overall level of economic activity within a UK region or sub-region. 'GVA per head' expresses that activity relative to the size of the resident population. What Table 5 shows is that on this measure, the economy of Wales is considerably weaker than that of any other part of the UK – and that it has been so for more than a decade.

Table 5: Gross Value Added per head, as a percentage of UK and in pounds

	1989 (% of UK)	1999 (% of UK)	2008 (% of UK)	2008 (£)
Wales	85%	77%	74%	£15,240
Northern Ireland	73%	79%	79%	£16,190
Scotland	96%	95%	98%	£20,090
England	102%	103%	102%	£21,020
- of which: North East	84%	78%	77%	£15,890

Source: Office for National Statistics, 2009, NUTS1 GVA, table 1.1. GVA per head indices are measured relative to the UK less extra regio. In this and subsequent tables, the English North East appears in its role as the poorest of the nine English regions.

At £15,240 per head in 2008, GVA was more than £600 lower than in the English North East (itself the weakest of the English regions) and nearly £1,000 lower than in Northern Ireland. The difference with Scotland was not far short of £5,000 while that with England as a whole was not far short of £6,000. As a proportion of the UK average, GVA per head in Wales was 74 per cent.

Looking back, the decline in Wales relative to the UK average was faster between 1989 and 1999 (down from 85 per cent to 77 per cent) than subsequently (down from 77 per cent to 74 per cent).[7] The decline in the first decade of the new century was not just a result of rapid growth in London and the English South East as can be seen from the way that GVA per head in Northern Ireland kept pace with the UK average while Scotland surpassed it.[8] Northern Ireland overtook Wales during the 1990s.

Although GVA is only one source of Welsh household income (the other main one being the social security and tax credits payments less taxes paid from the UK government), it is very important as a measure of Wales's capacity to generate its 'own' income. So at less than three quarters of the UK average, why is the Welsh figure so low?

The working and non-working populations

Part of the reason is that Wales has an unusually high proportion of its population who are not working. Since GVA per head is the value of economic activity performed by those in work, divided by the whole population, this obviously serves to reduce the Welsh figure. Table 6, which splits the population into three groups shows by how much. At just under 43 per cent, Wales – along with Northern Ireland – has the smallest share of its population in work, followed by the English North East on 44 per cent. The shortfall of more than three percentage points compared with the UK average is sufficient to account for about a quarter of Wales's low GVA per head.[9]

Wales has an unusually high proportion of its population who are not working

Table 6: Population shares by age and work status: 2008

	Under 16s and pension age	Non-working, working-age	Working, working-age
Wales	39.9%	17.3%	42.8%
Northern Ireland	38.2%	18.8%	43.0%
Scotland	37.4%	15.0%	47.6%
England	37.9%	15.7%	46.4%
- of which: North East	38.0%	18.5%	43.5%
UK	38.0%	15.8%	46.2%

Source: Office for National Statistics, 2010, Regional Trends, table 1.1a (under 16 and pension age) and Office for National Statistics, 2010, LFS Regional Summary (working-age).

There is another point of interest here. Of the two groups who make up the non-working population, those under 16 or over pension age actually contribute more to the difference from the UK average (1.9 per cent) than does the non-working, working-age group (1.5 per cent). Wales's pensioner population takes an especially large share (second only to that of the English South West). Given the attention that is paid to the high levels of unemployment and economic inactivity in Wales, it is surprising to find that on this measure at least, demography is actually more important.

Labour productivity

If stripping out the effect of the non-working population improves the picture by closing the gap somewhat between Wales and the UK average, it does nothing for the story about what has been happening over time. An official series that gets round the population effect by dividing GVA by the number of filled jobs – Table 7 – shows a fall in productivity since the late 1990s of approaching 1 per cent a year. While Northern Ireland, Scotland and the English North East also show declines, none do so on this scale. On this measure, Wales and Northern Ireland had the lowest levels of productivity of any UK region in 2008.

Table 7: Gross value added per job filled as a percentage of UK

	1999 (as % of UK)	2008 (as % of UK)
Wales	90.8%	84.0%
Northern Ireland	87.9%	84.0%
Scotland	97.5%	95.4%
England	101.1%	101.8%
- of which: North East	91.5%	87.9%

Source: Office for National Statistics, 2010, Regional Trends, table 3.2. This source also provides a second productivity measure in which GVA is divided by hours worked. Here the decline for Wales is almost as steep, down from 92.1% of the UK average in 1999 to 86.4% in 2008. One caveat should be born in mind. Unlike the 'headline' GVA figures in table 2.1, these series do sometimes move sharply from one year to the next. As a result, individual year's figures should be regarded as having a greater degree of uncertainty attached to them.).

Earnings

Stripped to its essentials, GVA is simply the sum of employee compensation and the gross operating surplus – in shorthand, wages and profits. While the latter varies between regions and over time, the former is much the bigger part and greater influence. Most of the explanation for Wales's low GVA lies in its low level of wages (or earnings): a mean value of 81.8 per cent of the UK average in 2008.[10] Although on this measure both Northern Ireland and the English North East have fractionally lower mean earnings, the difference is so small as to be insignificant, particularly since none of the other regions come remotely close. Alongside these two, Wales is unequivocally a low pay economy.

Wales is unequivocally a low pay economy

Table 8: Gross value added per job filled as a percentage of UK

	Median	*Mean*
Wales	87.4%	81.8%
Northern Ireland	87.4%	81.6%
Scotland	96.9%	91.0%
England		102.6%
- of which: North East	88.3%	81.5%

Source: Office for National Statistics, 2009, A Survey of Hours and Earnings, table 5.7a.

Earnings by industry

This message is strongly reinforced by the statistics at the industry level shown in Table 9 which shows that in all but one of the 19 sectors, both median and mean earnings are lower in Wales than in the UK as a whole. One consequence of this is that at this level the actual sectoral distribution of jobs in Wales produces a level of mean earnings which is almost identical to what it would be if the sectoral distribution followed the UK pattern.[11] The problem is not that Wales has too many jobs in low paying sectors (compared with the UK as a whole) but rather that pay is low across the board.[12]

The one exception to the general rule – health and social work – where both mean and median pay are a couple of percentage points higher than the UK average – is of little comfort since this is a low paying sector anyway, with median pay some 15 per cent less than the overall Wales median.

One other point in Table 9 relates to what is referred to there as the 'bias towards high pay jobs'. The data from which this table is drawn show that in every case, both in Wales and in the UK as a whole, mean pay – that is average pay across the sector – is higher than median pay – that is, the pay of the average worker in the sector. This situation is most likely to be due to a few employees at the top of the scale being paid a lot more than average.[13]

The last column in the table shows whether this bias is more or less pronounced in Wales. In most cases (whenever the statistic is less than one)

Table 9: Median and mean earnings by industrial sector: Wales as a percentage of UK: 2008

Industrial sector (ranked by Welsh employment size)	Median: Wales as % of UK	Mean: Wales as % of UK	Bias towards high pay jobs
Education	90%	95%	1.06
Human health and social work activities	102%	103%	1.01
Wholesale and Retail Trade	86%	77%	0.90
Manufacturing	95%	89%	0.93
Public Administration and Defence	82%	87%	1.06
Construction	86%	80%	0.94
Administrative and Support Service Activities	84%	73%	0.87
Accommodation and Food Service Activities	95%	80%	0.84
Financial and Insurance Activities	70%	51%	0.74
Professional, Scientific and Technical Activities	71%	65%	0.91
Transportation and storage	87%	86%	0.99
Information and communication	77%	70%	0.91
Other service activities	n/a	77%	n/a
Real estate activities	n/a	67%	n/a
Agriculture, forestry and fishing	n/a	73%	n/a
Mining and quarrying	n/a	n/a	n/a
Electricity, Gas, Steam And Air Conditioning Supply	n/a	86%	n/a
Water Supply; Sewerage, Waste Management etc	83%	77%	0.92

Source: Office for National Statistics, 2009, A Survey of Hours and Earnings, table 5.7a.

the bias is less in Wales, sometimes (e.g. finance and insurance) strikingly so. But there are three exceptions – education, public administration and health – and they are important, because they are in the public sector, because they are large and because the people receiving these high earnings are likely to be making decisions about the pay of many others. While it would be wrong to read too much into a few, fairly fragile statistics, they do suggest that the top end of the public sector has been able to protect itself a little against the general tendency for earnings to be so much lower in Wales than elsewhere.

Earnings by sex and by full- or part-time employment

To complete the picture, Table 10 shows median and mean hourly earnings separately for full-time male employees, full-time female employees and part-time employees.[14] Again, all three groups show markedly lower earnings, the percentages for Wales (compared with the UK) all lying in the 85 per cent to 95 per cent range. In all of this, Wales is very close to the English North East.

There are two other points here. First, the fact that part-time earnings in Wales are only a little below the UK average is not a sign of strength in the Welsh part-time labour market so much as the fact that part-time earnings are poor everywhere.

Table 10: Median and mean hourly earnings, male and female full-time and part-time: 2008

	Male full-time median	Male full-time mean	Female full-time median	Female full-time mean	Part-time median	Part-time mean
Wales: £ per hour	£11.40	£13.40	£9.80	£11.40	£13.40	£9.80
Wales: % of UK	90%	86%	89%	90%	86%	89%
Northern Ireland: % of UK	83%	81%	91%	83%	81%	91%
Scotland: % of UK	97%	93%	98%	97%	93%	98%
England: % of UK		102%			102%	
- of which: North East: % of UK	89%	84%	89%	89%	84%	89%

Source: Office for National Statistics, 2009, A Survey of Hours and Earnings, table 5.5a.

Second, both all three medians and all three means for Wales are slightly higher than the overall median and mean in Table 10.[15] This is a sign that compared with the UK, employment in Wales is shifted towards the lower paying jobs, that is, part-time rather than female full-time, and female full-time rather than male full-time. While this shift contributes towards a statistical explanation of Wales's lower overall pay, it is hardly an explanation in the full sense since it is just such a shift that itself needs explaining.

Gross Value Added per head across Wales

In the last part of this section, we return to the figures on GVA per head in order to show the degree of disparity in income generation across Wales. The data on which these figures rest are far too slight to bear the weight of any real analysis. Certainly, many of the factors considered above will contribute to the differences seen here, including variations in the mix by industrial sector, the male/female, full/part-time balance, the size of the non-working population and, especially in the case of Cardiff, the contribution to GVA coming from profits as opposed to earnings.

Besides the degree of disparity – a ratio of almost two to one between the highest (146 per cent in Cardiff and the Vale of Glamorgan) and the lowest (75 per cent in the Gwent Valleys), the other point of note here is the change since 1999. Restricting attention to the order of the twelve sub-regions only, here are really only two notable changes, namely the improving position of the South West, and the deterioration, to last place, of the Gwent Valleys (no doubt associated with the closure of the steel works in Ebbw Vale).

Table 11: GVA per head in 12 Welsh sub-regions as per cent of Wales average: 1999 and 2007

Sub-region	1999	2007	Change in rank 2007 cf 1999
Isle of Anglesey	66%	76%	+1
Gwynedd	85%	88%	+1
Conwy and Denbighshire	82%	81%	
South West Wales	77%	84%	+3
Central Valleys	79%	77%	
Gwent Valleys	84%	75%	-4
Bridgend and Neath Port Talbot	94%	94%	
Swansea	98%	104%	
Monmouthshire and Newport	134%	123%	
Cardiff and Vale of Glamorgan	136%	146%	
Flintshire and Wrexham	127%	116%	
Powys	93%	86%	-1

Source: Office for National Statistics, 2009, NUTS3 GVA per head, table 3.6. These more detailed statistics always published a year later than he higher level one – hence 2007 is still the latest year for which data is available.

Household income and wealth
Household income per head

If economic activity – gross value added – per head relative to the UK has been falling in Wales, what about household income? Has Wales been falling further behind there too? The answer (at least up until 2008) is 'certainly not'. Despite the awkward presentation due to the difficulty of finding a single series to cover the full period, Table 12 shows that relative to the UK average, Welsh household income per head rose slightly in the ten years up to 1999 and a good deal more substantially in the nine years thereafter. Although Northern Ireland has followed this path even more vigorously (and has overtaken Wales as a result), Welsh household income per head remains well above that in the English North East. While hardly strong, this is a more benign picture than anything seen so far.

Table 12: Disposable and gross disposable household income per head as a percentage of UK

	1989 (disposable)	1999 (disposable)	1999 (gross disposable)	2008 (gross disposable)
Wales	89.8%	90.4%	85.7%	87.9%
Northern Ireland	85.1%	85.9%	84.5%	89.2%
Scotland	96.3%	94.8%	93.0%	96.2%
England	101.5%	101.6%	102.1%	101.5%
- of which: North East	88.3%	82.9%	84.9%	84.3%

Source: Office for National Statistics, 2010, Regional Statistics, table 3.4 (gross household disposable income 1999 and 2008) and 2001, Regional Trends 36, table 12.7 (household disposable income 1989 and 1999).

The cause of the rise in household income relative to the UK appears to be the increasing contribution that has come from employment and self-employment (Table 13). In 1999, this paid work accounted for 68 per cent of Welsh household income compared with 75 per cent for the UK on average. By 2008, however, while the UK share had risen one percentage point, to 76 per cent, the share in Wales had risen five points to 73 per cent – still lower, but now much closer.

Table 13: Components of household income, Wales and UK: 1997-2000 and 2006-2008

	Wages and salaries	Self-employment	Investments	Annuities and pensions	Social security benefits	Other Income
UK 1997-2000	67%	8%	4%	7%	12%	1%
UK 2006-2008	67%	9%	4%	7%	13%	1%
Wales 1997-2000	61%	7%	4%	8%	19%	2%
Wales 2006-2008	64%	9%	3%	8%	15%	1%

Source: Office for National Statistics, 2010, Regional Statistics, table 8.1 (2006-2008) and 2001, Regional Trends 36, table 8.1 (1997-2000).

In turn, the rising share coming from work reflects the rise in employment over the same period, up 10 per cent from 1.2 million in 1999 to 1.33m in 2008. The employment rate (among those of working age) rose over the same period from 68.7 per cent to 70.7 per cent.[16]

Households receiving social security benefits

Although the proportion of household income in the form of social security benefits has gone down in Wales (Table 14), it remains the case that at 74 per cent, Wales (alongside Northern Ireland) is second only to the English North East in the proportion of households in receipt of such benefits.[17]

Table 14: Households in receipt of social security benefits, 2007/08.

	Pension Credits	Tax Credits	Housing Benefit	Council Tax Benefit	JSA	Retirement Pension benefits	Disability benefits	Any
Wales	14%	17%	14%	22%	3%	33%	22%	74%
Northern Ireland:	16%	20%	15%		3%	27%	23%	74%
Scotland	14%	17%	17%	22%	2%	30%	18%	70%
England	13%	17%	14%	19%	2%	30%	15%	70%
- of which: North East	20%	20%	21%	28%	4%	31%	22%	76%
UK	13%	17%	14%	19%	2%	30%	16%	70%

Source: Office for National Statistics, 2010, Regional Statistics, table 8.7. 'Any benefit' also includes Child Benefit

Where Wales stands alone in this table is in the 33 per cent of households receiving the State Retirement Pension. But where Wales, along with the English North East and Northern Ireland differ most from the UK average is in the 22 per cent receiving disability benefits – in effect, a third more than the average.[18] A key point about most of these benefits, along with Income Support (for working-age people), Jobseeker's Allowance and the State Retirement Pension, is that the value of these benefits has only been up-rated over time in line with prices. Had they instead gone up with earnings since (say) 1999, they would have been worth some 20 per cent more by 2008 than they actually were.

The effect of high and low household incomes on the overall average

Average gross household income in Wales – £570 a week in 2008 – was equal to 85 per cent of the UK figure (Table 15). This was the second lowest proportion after the English North East (81 per cent). Almost inevitably, a low average like this reflects both an over-abundance of very low income households (compared with the UK) and a shortage of very high income ones. The question is, however, whether they are both more or less responsible or whether one of the two is much the more important.

Table 15 divides households into three groups according to their weekly gross income, namely less than £250, £250 to £1,000, or more than £1,000. With its 29 per cent of households getting less than £250 and 14 per cent getting more than £1,000, Wales has a higher proportion of the former and a smaller proportion of the latter than any other UK region bar the English North East.

Table 15: The distribution of household incomes 2006 to 1008; averages as a percentage of UK

	Distribution of households by gross weekly income			Average gross weekly income as % of UK		
	Less than £250	£250 to £1,000	More than £1,000	All	Excluding incomes of less than £150	Excluding incomes of more than £1000
Wales	29%	57%	14%	85%	86%	94%
Northern Ireland:	24%	59%	17%	92%	91%	100%
Scotland	26%	57%	17%	92%	93%	97%
England	23%	56%	20%	102%	101%	101%
- of which: North East	31%	58%	12%	81%	83%	94%
UK	24%	56%	19%	£671	100%	100%

Source: Office for National Statistics, 2010, Regional Statistics, tables 8.1 and 8.2 Final two columns: estimates assume £100 for those on less than £150 and mid point for all other income groups.

The effect on the average of the two ends of the income distribution can be estimated to a good degree of accuracy from the published data. The last two columns in the table show the estimates. Excluding household incomes below £150 (last but one column) does little to alter the overall average, lifting it from 85 per cent to just 86 per cent in Wales and by slightly more in the English North East. By contrast, excluding household incomes above £1,000 (last column) makes a big difference, lifting both Wales and the English North East to 94 per cent of the UK average and Northern Ireland all the way to 100 per cent. While Wales and the English North East still have lowest averages, the difference from the UK is some two thirds lower if high incomes are excluded. The clear conclusion: low average household income in Wales is largely to do with a shortage of very high income households rather than an abundance of very low incomes ones.

The distribution of individual incomes

Averaging household incomes like this takes no account of household size. Counting individuals according to their 'equivalised' household income is a well-established way round this problem.15 Table 16, which shows the distribution of individual incomes on this basis, further reinforces the impression that the main way in which Wales differs from the average is in having relatively few high incomes rather than relatively many low income ones. As well as being slightly over-represented in the bottom fifth (21 per cent of individuals), Wales like the English North East is also over-represented in the second and third fifths too (23 per cent and 22 per cent). They are then correspondingly under-represented in the top fifth.

Income calculated on this basis is how poverty rates are calculated. That the Welsh income distribution is similar to the UK's except at the top implies that the extent of poverty in Wales is likely to be worse, but only a little so, than the UK average. The poverty statistics, given in the final column of the table, confirm this to be so, with Wales and the English North East having poverty rate 24 per cent, compared with 22 per cent for England (and 23 per cent for the UK as a whole).

Table 16: The distribution of individual incomes by fifths of the UK income distribution, and the poverty rate 2005/06 to 2007/08

	Lowest quintile	2nd lowest	Middle quintile	2nd highest	Highest quintile	Poverty rate
Wales	21%	23%	22%	19%	15%	24%
Northern Ireland:	18%	24%	23%	20%	15%	20%
Scotland	17%	20%	21%	22%	20%	19%
England	20%	20%	20%	20%	21%	22%
- of which: North East	21%	22%	23%	19%	14%	24%

Source: Office for National Statistics, 2010, Regional Statistics, table 8.3 and Department for Work and Pensions, Households Below Average Income 2009, table 3.6. All figures on an 'after housing costs' basis.

Low incomes across Wales

In the absence of reliable statistics on household or individual incomes in different parts of Wales, data on those receiving different kinds of social security benefits and tax credits can be used as a proxy. Table 17 uses two such proxies, namely: the proportion of the working-age population receiving a key out-of-work benefit; and the proportion of families receiving child and/or working tax credits. In each case, the table shows the five areas with the highest proportions relative to the overall Welsh average, and the three with the lowest.

Table 17: Welsh local authorities with the highest and lowest proportions receiving certain benefits, as a percentage of the all-Wales average, 2009

Proportion receiving a key out-of-work benefit		Proportion receiving child/working tax credits	
Highest five		**Highest five**	
Merthyr Tydfil	151%	Conwy	113%
Blaenau Gwent	148%	Ceredigion	111%
Neath Port Talbot	133%	Merthyr Tydfil	108%
Caerphilly	128%	Carmarthenshire	107%
Rhondda Cynon Taf	127%	Blaenau Gwent	107%
Lowest three		**Lowest three**	
Powys	70%	Monmouthshire	89%
Monmouthshire	68%	Cardiff	88%
Ceredigion	63%	The Vale of Glamorgan	85%

Source: Office for National Statistics, 2010, Regional Statistics, tables 8.8 and 10.2. Calculation of the second statistics uses the population aged under 16 as the denominator. Key out-of-work benefits include Jobseeker's Allowance, Income Support, Employment and Support Allowance, Incapacity Benefit, Severe Disablement Allowance

Two points stand out here. The first is that the geographical patterns are very different between the two cases. While the South Wales Valley authorities dominate the out-of-work benefit measure, West Wales authorities occupy three of the five top places on the tax credit measure. The second is that the degree of variation is much greater on the out-of-work benefit measure (varying from 63 per cent of the all-Wales average in Ceredigion to 151 per cent in Merthyr Tydfil) than on the tax credit measure (85 per cent in Vale of Glamorgan to 113 per cent in Conwy). With tax credits going both to those in working and non-working families, the latter measure will in part be reflecting the incidence of low income in work as well as low income out-of-work among families with dependent children.

Wealth in Wales

To complete the picture, Table 18 presents information on household wealth in Wales compared with other parts of Great Britain. Household wealth is made up of four elements, namely net property wealth, physical wealth, net financial wealth and private pension wealth. The table shows both median wealth – that held by the average household (£206,000 in 2006-08) – and mean wealth – the average over all households in Wales (£356,000 in 2006-08).

Table 18: Median and mean household wealth: 2006-08

	Median	*Mean*
Wales	£206,000	£356,000
Northern Ireland	100%	97%
Scotland	74%	92%
England		101%
- of which: North East	83%	82%

Source: Office for National Statistics, 2009, Wealth in Great Britain, tables 2.11 and 2.5.

Total wealth with pension wealth is the sum of: (i) net property wealth; (ii) physical wealth; (iii) net financial wealth; and (iv) private pension wealth. In their turn: (i) net property wealth is the sum of all property values minus value of all mortgages and value of amounts owed as a result of equity release; (ii) physical wealth is the sum of values of household contents, collectables and valuables, and vehicles; (iii) net financial wealth is the sum of formal and informal financial assets, assets held in the names of children and endowments purchased to repay mortgages less current account overdrafts, amounts owed on cards mail order, hire purchase, loans and arrears; and (iv) private pension wealth is the sum of current occupational pension wealth, retained rights in occupational pensions, current personal pension wealth, retained rights in personal pensions, AVCs, value of pensions expected from former spouse or partner and value of pensions in payment.

That the mean is so much higher than the median is not surprising, reflecting as it does the concentration of wealth towards the top end. With a Gini coefficient of 0.61, wealth in GB is much more concentrated than income.[20] What is surprising, however, is how high wealth is in Wales, with a median equal to the GB median and a mean just 97 per cent of the GB mean. These levels are way above those in both Scotland and the English North East.

The likely explanation for the relatively high median is Wales's high proportion of owner occupiers, some 73 per cent of all dwellings in 2007, above the UK and England averages (70 per cent in both cases) and well above those for Scotland and the English North East (65 per cent in both cases).[21]

Conclusion

Thirty years ago in a similar survey to this, Paul Wilding said this:

"A study of the pattern of earnings in Wales suggests no particular problem of deprivation relative to earnings levels in Britain. A study of incomes, on the other hand, shows that Wales is an area of very considerable deprivation relative to England, the United Kingdom or any of the English regions.[22]"

What is striking about this conclusion is that it is the opposite of the one reached here. Here the income picture is quite benign. Although the child poverty statistics have been very disappointing for several years, this is a UK-wide problem rather than one particular to Wales. Over the period, indeed, Wales has moved closer to the UK average. Pensioner poverty is down sharply and the rate in Wales is identical to the UK average. Gross disposable household income has risen relative to the UK and although still low on average, this is more to do with a shortage of high income households than an overabundance of low income ones. Once allowance is made for household size, the over-representation of low income households is about one part in twenty. On household wealth, the level and distribution in Wales is very similar to the UK. By contrast, Gross Value Added per head and labour productivity have long been falling relative to the UK average. Both of these, along with median and mean earnings are as low as anywhere in the UK. This was not the position 30 years ago and is evidently not so benign at all.

The future depends on the answers to two key questions.

> **how has this conjunction of weak economic and earnings performance and a stronger income performance come about?**

First, how has this conjunction of weak economic and earnings performance and a stronger income performance come about? Are weak earnings and stronger income permanently compatible – or does the sharp rise in worklessness that has already taken place (but not yet fed through to the income statistics) and the new era of fiscal austerity (the prospects for out-of-work benefits and tax credits on which so many in Wales depend, as well as the possibility of cuts in employment in the public sector) mean that the path followed over the last decade goes no further? If they are not compatible, a new route will be needed which will surely have to pay as much attention to the quality of jobs and what they are worth as to the mere quantity of them.

Second, what is the connection between the failure to sustain the earlier progress on poverty and what has happened to overall income inequality? The table in the introduction showed three measures of income inequality across the UK in the mid 1990s at all-time highs. Yet by the end of the 21st century's first decade, they had all risen further still, especially the measure of inequality in the lower half (the 50:10 ratio) and the overall measure of inequality including the extremes below 10 per cent and above 90 per cent (the Gini coefficient)[23]. Even if Wales continues to restrict its goals in this area to the reduction of poverty, it hardly seems possible that overall income inequality can continue, for much longer, to be ignored.

1 Median income is the income of the (in this case) individual in the very middle of the distribution – that is, half the population has an income higher than this person and half has one that is lower. The key thing about the median is that in arithmetical terms, it does not matter how high or low the extremes are. So if the person at the top of the income distribution saw their income go up from £10 million to £100 million, it would not change the median at all. When measured in relation to median income, 'poverty' therefore boils down to how far away people on low incomes are from income in the middle.

2 Wilding, P., 1980, "Income and Wealth in Wales", in *Poverty and Social Inequality in Wales*, G. and T. L. Rees (eds), Croom Helm.

3 For example, data for the financial year 2008/09 was only published in May 2010, a delay which has been the norm for several years now. Assuming this pattern continues in 2011, child poverty for the three years 2006/07 to 2008/09 will still be the latest available when the next Assembly elections are fought in May 2011. At the time of that election, therefore, the latest official figures will refer to an average circa October 2007, something over which the outgoing Assembly Government in 2011 will have had almost no impact. For evidence of the wild swings in the Welsh numbers, see footnote 5.

4 To give this measure its shorthand description, AHC or 'After Housing Cost'.

5 What these three year averages disguise is the huge movement year to year in the recent child poverty rate: 31%, 36% and 27% in the three latest years. With no good reason for this scale of variation, there must be serious doubts about the adequacy of the underlying statistical sampling.

6 Source: Department for Work and Pensions, 2010, *Households Below Average Income*, table 4.5ts.

7 That this is part of a longer term trend can be seen from the fact that in 1976, the broadly comparable GDP per head for Wales was 89% (Wilding, op cit: p34). Over the decade prior to that (that is, from the mid 1960s), Wilding reports the proportion as having fluctuated in the range 83% to 89%.

8 Interpretation of Scottish statistics up to about 2008 must always be treated with caution in view of the exceptional experience in that country over the three years prior to the recession compared with England or Wales.

9 So if Wales had 46% of its population in work (the UK average) instead of 43%, its GVA per head would be about six percentage points higher at around 80%.

10 The proportion made up of profit varies across the UK regions between about 37% and 44% of the total (Source: Office for National Statistics, 2009, *NUTS1 GVA*, table 1.9.). While a full explanation of Wales' low GVA per head would need to take variations in this component into account, their small size (especially over the last decade and in comparison with the UK average) means that this is a level of detail which it is not necessary to go into here.

11 Source: author's calculation using data from *A Survey of Hours and Earnings*, 2009, table 5.7a.

12 This is not to say that the distribution (or structure) of employment at lower level is not making any difference. For example, gross earnings vary more than twofold as between different sub-sectors of manufacturing. Clearly, therefore it can make a great deal of difference to overall earnings exactly where the jobs sit within this or indeed other sectors.

13 For example, suppose that the highest paid person in a sector sees their pay double. This has no effect on median pay (the worker in the middle of the pay distribution is the same worker as before, and his or her pay has not changed). By contrast, mean pay – that is, total pay averaged over all workers – will have gone up.

14 The reason for treating male and female part-time workers as one here is that there is insufficient data on the former to give a complete. Based on the UK data, however, two things can be said. First, on the basis of the similarity between their median earnings, male part-time employees are as likely to be low paid as female part-time employees. By contrast, male part-time mean earnings do tend to be higher, suggestive of the fact that the proportion of male part-timers who are well paid is greater than the proportion of women part-timers.

15 Although table 2.4 relates to gross annual earnings as opposed to gross hourly earnings as here, the key observation – that all individual medians exceeds the overall median – is true for the gross annual data in just the same way.

16 Source: Labour Force Survey, four quarter average December 1998 to November 1999 (via Nomis) and Office for National Statistics, 2010, *Labour Market Statistics Wales*, table 2.

17 In 1999, this proportion was 76%: Office for National Statistics, 2001, *Regional Trends 36*, table 8.8.

18 Disability benefits comprise: Incapacity Benefit, Disability Living Allowance (Care and Mobility components), Severe Disablement Allowance, Industrial Injuries Disablement Benefit, War Disablement Pension and Attendance Allowance and the disability element of Working Tax Credit.

19 'Equivalisation' uses internationally determined weights to try to reflect the fact that while two people need more income than one to reach the same standard of living, they do not need twice as much.

20 Office for National Statistics, 2009, *Wealth in Great Britain*, page xxi.

21 Source: Office for National Statistics, 2010, *Regional Statistics*, table 7.3.

22 Wilding, P., 1980, "Income and Wealth in Wales", p41, in *Poverty and Social Inequality in Wales*, G. and T. L. Rees (eds), Croom Helm.

23 The latest figures, along with the ones for the mid 1990s for comparison, are as follows (see first table for notes):

1994/95-1996/97	2.33	2.13	0.37
2006/07 to 2008/09	2.45	2.14	0.40

2.

ASPECTS
of
Poverty

Child **poverty** in Wales:
Where there's the will, **is there a way?**
Sean O'Neill

THE FIGHT AGAINST CHILD POVERTY has become a growing priority for Governments across most European member states over recent decades. This has been reflected in social, economic and regeneration policies and programmes designed to help tackle the root causes of child poverty, or at least attempt to alleviate some of the adverse consequences for children. In the most recent reports on National Strategies for Social Protection and Social Inclusion, the majority of European countries have outlined cross-cutting strategies and systems to help prevent and address child poverty and social exclusion levels. The UK National Action Plan, for example, outlines the Government's key priority of combating child poverty and the policies designed to achieve this, as well as highlighting areas where improvements have been made. The EU Year for Combating Poverty and Social Exclusion 2010 has provided further impetus to the need for all nation states to make greater headway in reducing the number of children persistently disadvantaged through poverty and exclusion, which amount to around 20 million. This reflects the continued concern that children in the European Union are at greater risk of living in poverty than any other section of our societies (Frazer, Marlier and Nicaise 2010). In the UK, children are still much more likely to live in low-income households than the population as a whole: 31 per cent compared to 22 per cent.

> **children are still much more likely to live in low-income households than the population as a whole**

Since the advent of the welfare state, the attention given to childhood poverty by successive UK governments has fluctuated. Through the 'rediscovery of poverty' discourse and lectures of the late Peter Townsend and other notable scholars during the 1960s and 1970s, it became clear that the welfare state had not provided the 'safety net' for families in times of unemployment and worklessness as was initially intended. Although child poverty rates were relatively low compared to more recent times, questions were beginning to be asked as to whether the Beveridge model was adequate to protect children and families from the economic cycle of boom and bust. In the 1980s and 1990s, child poverty rates in the UK reached unprecedented levels, reflecting high unemployment and turbulence in global markets. Something clearly had to be done.

With the arrival and fanfare of the UK Labour Government in 1997 came much hope and expectation that change was on the horizon and that political attention would shortly turn to the need to seek solutions for the growing number of children living in low-income and disadvantaged households. The then Prime Minister Tony Blair confirmed this optimism with an address in March 1999 which made clear that:

'Our historic aim will be for ours to be the first generation to end child poverty'.

The stage was set for the elimination of child poverty. National targets were soon developed benchmarked against child poverty levels of 1998/99: there was a commitment to reduce the number in poverty by 25 per cent by 2005, to halve it by 2010 and to eradicate child poverty entirely by 2020. Not only did the country finally have recognition by a Government of its role and responsibility in addressing the plight of so many children and families across the UK, these national targets provided economists, lobbyists and children's organisations alike with milestones with which they could track progress and hold Government to account.

> **it is dispiriting that the rhetoric has so far failed to deliver the desired outcomes. Statistically, child poverty remains stubbornly high**

Meanwhile, in Wales, there was widespread support for this new drive and commitment to tackle child poverty, the UK Government targets soon being supported by the Welsh Assembly Government. In June 2004, the then Minister for Children reaffirmed the Welsh Assembly Government position by stating that:

'The Welsh Assembly Government strongly believes that child poverty should be eradicated within a generation'

Similar statements have been made by successive ministers responsible for the child poverty portfolio. The present coalition Government's *One Wales Agreement* (2007) re-states the goal of eradicating child poverty and a determination to improve the life chances of the poorest and most vulnerable throughout Wales.

However, despite both the UK and Welsh Governments' commitments to eradicating child poverty being in place, the support of all the major opposition parties, and a whole raft of policies and programmes to achieve the goal, it is dispiriting that the rhetoric has so far failed to deliver the desired outcomes. Statistically, child poverty remains stubbornly high.

Keeping the promise: child poverty levels

Modern definitions of poverty in developed countries have moved away from those based on lack of physical necessities (absolute poverty) towards a social and relative understanding. Poverty is also not solely about income, but about the effective exclusion of people from ordinary living patterns, customs and activities. Measurements of poverty therefore seek to reflect a standard of living, determined principally by levels of income whilst also including material deprivation and other aspects of well-being such as health, education, housing, participation, financial support and safety. This is in recognition of the different and interrelated ways in which poverty impacts on children and families, and how badly the UK has done in developing a multifaceted response in relation to other relatively wealthy countries (UNICEF Child Well Being Report).

In relation to the principal measurement, income, Government statistics consider relative income levels, which allow for comparisons to be made across different regions, between the four nations of the UK as well as with EU neighbour states. Children are considered to be living in poverty when their household's income is below 60 per cent of national median income after deducting housing costs. This equates to approximately £247 per week for a lone parent with two children aged 5 and 14 and £333 for a couple household with two children aged 5 and 14.

On this measure, levels of child poverty grew quite rapidly throughout the 1980s and early 1990s with a peak of almost 4.5 million children living in low-income households when the Labour Party came to power. Although encouraging progress was made between 1998/99 and 2004/05 when the overall figure fell to 3.7 million, child poverty rates have increased steadily each year since. The most recent data available (August 2009) for the period 2007/08 show that there were 4 million children in poverty, around 31 per cent of all children in the UK.

> **the UK has comparatively high levels of child poverty compared to other western nations**

At a European level, the UK has comparatively high levels of child poverty compared to other western nations, with only Poland, Italy and Greece having higher rates of child poverty than the UK (Eurostat 2008). Although care should be taken when examining cross-country comparisons, the UK is far from a shining example to others. Rates of child poverty are consistently lower across Scandinavia and other comparable wealthy European states.

At a regional level, Chart 1 shows the proportion of children in low-income households (after housing costs) in parts of the UK. Wales has

Chart 1: Proportion of Children in Low-Income Households (after housing costs) by Region, 1995/96 and 2007/08

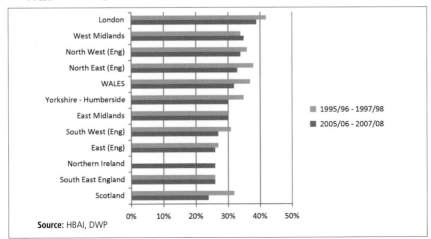

Source: HBAI, DWP

followed similar patterns to other parts of the UK in terms of recording a promising decrease in the number of children living in poverty during the early part of the last decade. There has however been a steady increase since 2004/05, with most of the progress on reducing child poverty levels to this date being lost (New Policy Institute 2010). According to most recent figures, around 200,000 children and young people now live in low-income households in Wales – 32 per cent. Wales has amongst the highest rates of child poverty in the UK and the highest amongst all the devolved nations. Given the present fiscal challenges and sharp rise in unemployment this figure is projected to rise even further.

Overall, whilst the commitment by Governments to the eradication of child poverty by 2020 still stands (at the time of writing this article at least) the milestones to achieve the target have all been missed, and the number of children living in low-income households remains above the Government target for 2004/5.

So what are the challenges we face in Wales?

Wales shares many of the challenges that neighbouring countries face in tackling child poverty, yet there is a growing sense, backed up by figures, that Wales has fared particularly badly. This is especially true when examining child poverty rates at a local level with many former industrial and manufacturing areas, such as the south Wales valleys, and areas of northeast Wales previously reliant on tourism faring particularly badly. This underlines Wales's vulnerability to change, such as that in the 1980s. The legacy of that era, coupled with more recent pressures, makes tackling child poverty over the next decade all the more difficult. Unemployment levels are currently higher than in both England and Scotland, and this is before the public expenditure cuts announced by the Chancellor have taken effect.

Risk factors for child poverty are many. According to the Households Below Average Income Survey (August 2009):

- 56 per cent of children live in families where at least one adult is in paid work.
- Over 40 per cent of the children in low-income households are residing in lone parent families.
- Unemployment remains a major risk factor for low income.
- Around half of unemployed people are young adults (18-24).

Living in a family where there is no one working remains the biggest risk factor

There is also a greater risk of poverty if a child lives with a disabled parent, lives in a large family, is of Pakistani or Bangladeshi origin, has had some experience of state care or is an asylum seeker (Waldfogel 2010).

Living in a family where there is no one working remains the biggest risk factor. This is particularly damaging for children where adults find themselves away from the labour market for long periods of time and claiming long-term benefits. Children not only grow up in households where no one works but also in communities where work is scarce and where a large proportion of households are reliant on state benefits. Where successive generations have not worked, there can be a detrimental impact on children in relation to motivation and aspirations for the future. One of the greatest challenges is the attempt to break inter-generational cycles of poverty and re-engage children and adults with education, training and employment.

More than half of children in low-income households live in families where at least one adult is in paid employment (56 per cent). In-work poverty has increased significantly since 2004/05. The recognition that work alone is not the solution to child poverty is nothing new, but Government rhetoric and policy have been slow to react. Whilst both the UK Child Poverty Act (2010) and forthcoming Welsh Assembly Government Child Poverty Strategy and Delivery Plan have acknowledged that in-work poverty needs to be addressed, it is not until the responsibility of employers to act is made more explicit that we can be confident that change is on the horizon. Though the Labour Government's introduction of a National Minimum Wage was welcome (despite the anomaly where younger employees get a lower rate for doing the same tasks), serious attention now needs to be given to the 'living wage' and 'minimum income standard' for Wales (see JRF July 2008).

> **it is not until the responsibility of employers to act is made more explicit that we can be confident that change is on the horizon**

What is being done about child poverty?

Given the devolution settlement for Wales, the drivers for change do not solely rest with one Government alone. Though the Welsh Assembly Government has direct control and considerable power over many social policy areas, including health and education, the majority of actions required to address income poverty, notably in and out-of-work benefit levels and taxation, rest with the government in Westminster. A dual approach is therefore demanded, as neither the UK nor the Welsh Assembly Government has the sufficient leverage to tackle child poverty in its broadest sense alone.

UK

At a UK level, a raft of policies and programmes was put in place largely based around the premise of paid employment and economic stability as being the best route out of poverty. A number of fiscal initiatives were introduced, most notably Working and Child Tax Credits, childcare support, the Child Trust Fund, increased levels of universal Child Benefit and the National Minimum Wage, along with actions such as New Deal work programmes, revamped Job Centre and Careers support as well as reform of welfare to work. 'Making work pay' and 'conditionality' of welfare support were seen as the golden solutions to child poverty. When demand for labour was high, such solutions achieved encouraging results, with falling levels of child poverty. However, it is much less clear if such measures can work in a slacker labour market. The current Government's abolition of Child Trust Funds, changes to Working and Child Tax Credits, changes to Child Benefit and Housing Benefit and further welfare reforms will all have an impact on children too.

In spring 2009, the Child Poverty Act 2010 placed a duty on Ministers to produce a national strategy setting out the policy and progress towards the 2020 child poverty target. Targets have been set for relative poverty, material deprivation, absolute low income and persistent poverty, with the UK Government now required to report progress annually. The Act has coincided with improved levels of cooperation between Governments with the creation of a four-nations joint child poverty unit of officials – essential given the complexity of the devolved powers within each of the different administrations.

Wales

Ministers have set about focusing on the policy areas in which they could make a real difference
Though it is generally accepted that the Welsh Assembly Government lacks the necessary power and leverage to tackle child poverty alone, Ministers have set about focusing on the policy areas in which they could make a real difference to the daily struggles of many low-income families. The Government's 2005 Child Poverty Strategy, 'A Fair Future for Our Children', underpinned by the UNCRC framework, was structured around three dimensions:

Income poverty – income maximisation, financial support and access to employment

Service poverty – enhancing access to and availability of core services alongside developing a programme of targeted services

Participation poverty – increasing the engagement of parents and children in a range of social and leisure activities, by promoting opportunities and addressing exclusion

A Phase 1 Implementation Plan (2006) soon followed which included commitments to 'child poverty-proof' all Welsh Assembly Government policies and programmes, in addition to emphasising the concept of 'programme bending' to ensure that resources and services are sufficiently targeted at those who could most benefit from them. In October of the same year, a series of measurable milestones and targets were set out in 'Eradicating Poverty – Measuring Success', centred on four major policy areas – Income/Work, Education, Health and Housing. An annual Statistical Bulletin provides an assessment of the progress made to date. Finally, in February 2008 a Ministerial Statement (Welsh Assembly Government, 2008) outlined

Table 1: Examples of initiatives

Policy, programme or initiative	Aim or Action
Communities First	Targeted support to aid regeneration of the most deprived communities in Wales
Cymorth Grant Scheme	Funding for services and programmes in pre-determined areas
Flying Start	Programme for families with children under 4 in disadvantaged areas – health visiting, parenting programmes and childcare
Genesis Wales	Support and advice for parents to access childcare and to help address other barriers to work
Children and Young People's Well being Monitor for Wales	Provides an overview on different aspects of the wellbeing of children and young people
Community Focused Schools	To provide a range of services and activities beyond the school day
Financial Inclusion Strategy	Income maximisation, affordable credit and savings
Credit Unions	Investment to establish a credit union in every local authority to increase access to financial services
Fuel Poverty Strategy	To address growing levels of fuel poverty amongst vulnerable households and support energy efficiency measures
10-year Homelessness Plan	Prevent homelessness and improve the conditions of people in temporary accommodation
Child Poverty Expert Group	Independent panel of experts established as an advisory body for Government
Free Swimming Schemes	Free swimming for children provided in school holidays
Free School Breakfast Scheme	Free Breakfast. All primary schools in Wales may participate if they wish
Breastfeeding Strategy – 'Investing in a Better Start'	To increase breastfeeding rates in Wales
National Oral Health Action Plan for Wales	To improve oral health
ASSIST Peer support programme	To encourage young people to not smoke and educate them of the risks
Families First Model	Pioneers areas recently announced to provide integrated and holistic support for families (presently being developed)
Basic Skills Strategy	To reduce the gap in achievement of literacy and numeracy
Skills that Work for Wales Strategy	To raise skill and employment levels across Wales
Our Healthy Future	To improve health outcomes for people in Wales
School Counselling Services	Counselling services available in schools to enable children and young people to access support and advice
Food and Fitness Strategy	Promote healthy eating and physical activity
Appetite for Life	Healthy Eating, including nutrition and school meals
Free or subsidised entry to cultural and heritage sites	To enable greater access by reducing or eliminating cost

the 'Three Strand Approach' to tackling child poverty, consisting of:
- Improving life opportunities for disadvantaged children
- Financial inclusion initiatives and
- Encouraging greater uptake of the UK tax and benefits support.

Whilst it is not the intention of this article to provide a comprehensive list of all the policies and activities that tackle child poverty, examples of key initiatives are in Table 1.

In addition, there are broader education programmes worth noting, such as the Foundation Phase, the School Effectiveness Framework and Learning Pathways 14-19, all designed to improve the educational outcomes of the poorest children whilst also seeking to enhance the learning opportunities and attainment level of all pupils throughout Welsh schools.

Recognition should also be given to the number of anti-poverty initiatives which are area based, accessible to all children and families located within pre-determined geographical locations. These include Communities First, Flying Start and the network of Integrated Children's Centres. The type and quality of service can vary enormously between different programmes. Although some disadvantaged children and families living within the designated area may benefit, those who live outside them will not. This has been a source of much debate, with the recognition that scarce resources need to be channelled to the most vulnerable at the same time as excluding some low-income families from support proving challenging.

Two recent developments are worth noting in some detail:

The Children and Families (Wales) Measure 2010

Using its new law-making powers, the Welsh Assembly Government's Children and Families (Wales) Measure 2010 provides a real opportunity for a joined up approach across all key stakeholders and partners. In addition to placing a statutory duty on Welsh Ministers to produce and publish a revised child poverty strategy, the Measure also requires local authorities, Local Health Boards and a range of named public bodies in Wales to set out the actions they will take at a local level to tackle child poverty. The Measure requires effort to focus on thirteen 'Broad Aims', a series of cross-cutting, all-encompassing objectives. It is clearly too soon to determine how successful the Measure will be in achieving the Government's goal, yet great strides have already been made in prioritising child poverty.

Child Poverty Strategy and Delivery Plan

In line with the duty outlined in the Children and Families (Wales) Measure, the Welsh Assembly Government issued their draft child poverty strategy and delivery plan for consultation during the summer of 2010. This three-part publication utilised the seven Core Aims (adapted from the UNCRC) as the framework for its planned priorities and actions as outlined in the Delivery Plan, supported by three overarching objectives:

1. To reduce the number of families living in workless households.

2. To improve the skill level of parents and young people in low income families so that they can secure well paid employment.

3. To reduce the inequalities that exist in the health, education and economic outcomes for children living in poverty, by improving the outcomes of the poorest.

The draft strategy has been broadly welcomed across the children's sector and should help to ensure that all partners see action to tackle child poverty as a joint priority. Seeking to ensure that other key bodies play their part is an aim worth supporting, though further work will be required around the role of schools (ECPN 2006).

> **Seeking to ensure that other key bodies play their part is an aim worth supporting**

The final strategy is due to be published in late 2010 at the earliest, and so it is far too soon to be confident that it will provide the impetus for change so desperately needed. However, with an emphasis on cross-departmental working, policy integration and strategic co-ordination, ensuring that all Welsh Ministers and officials take responsibility for monitoring the impact of policies in their brief, we can at least be somewhat assured that every effort is being made internally within the Welsh Assembly Government to address the weaknesses and gaps. Tough and unprecedented challenges lie immediately ahead. Whether or not the expectations and actions outlined in forthcoming delivery plan will be strong enough to withstand the UK Government's spending review, only time will tell.

Can more be done in Wales?

The journey towards the eradication of child poverty has stalled, at best, testament that a fresh approach is urgently needed. Greater pressure on public expenditure coupled with a rise in joblessness suggests that child poverty levels are likely to increase further in future. Governments must not only act now to protect the vulnerable and the services they so heavily rely on, but also show courage and leadership, so that despite the economic challenges ahead tackling poverty remains a priority. It is vital that the current generation of children are not made to pay the price and suffer as a consequence of the actions of a minority during the past decade. There is also a need to engage public support in this process (Hanley 2009).

In their response to the recent Welsh Assembly Government's draft child poverty strategy and delivery plan, the End Child Poverty Network Cymru identified a number of areas that require special attention in addition to those already identified by the Government in its draft publication.

Childcare

Accessible and affordable childcare is essential if parents are able to access employment, education or training opportunities, yet the gap between supply and demand has been well documented, especially for disabled children. With the relentless drive by the UK Government to get more people into work set to continue, a greater sense of urgency is needed from the Welsh Assembly Government to address the shortage of childcare, particularly for low-income families who do not benefit from provision provided through the Flying Start and other schemes. Despite the statutory duties placed on local authorities to secure sufficient childcare places for parents who want to work or train (Childcare Act 2006), many parents are either struggling to access childcare at a level they can afford or find that the cost of childcare outweighs any financial benefit they would expect to gain from being in employment. Childcare availability for children of primary and secondary school age is also patchy, as is care for children during school holidays.

Child Rights Based Framework

Central to the child poverty approach presently being pursued in Wales is the concerted focus on improving the life chances and opportunities of parents and adult family members. Whilst there is clearly a need to break the cycle of inter-generational poverty and deprivation in families by supporting parents, there are a number of risks when applying this approach to child poverty. In particular, there is a real danger that we begin to lose sight of the child.

Getting parents into any job is not always best for children. Parenting can become inferior due to the challenges of balancing work with family life, which leads to increased stress and friction in the home as well as less time for interaction between parent and child. When considering childcare for instance, we need to be satisfied that arrangements are in the best interest of the child (Article 3 of the UNCRC) as opposed to the best interests of the labour market. Equally, applying sanctions and cuts in benefits for lone parents who fail to comply with benefit regulations is clearly at odds with a child rights framework, as children are routinely punished for actions which are beyond their control. There is a need to ensure that the 'best interest and wishes and feeling of the child' principles are completely upheld.

In an attempt to overcome these potential challenges, it is suggested that a **Child's Rights Framework** is adopted which demands that the child is seen as the main actor and focus of considerations when decisions are being made. Delivering such an approach and positive outcomes for children would build on and be consistent with the Welsh Assembly Government's present commitment to the UNCRC when developing policies and programmes more generally. It would also support the view that child poverty is an infringement of the rights of children and the child's entitlement

> **There is a need to ensure that the 'best interest and wishes and feeling of the child' principles are completely upheld**

to live a life free of poverty. The proposed Rights of Children and Young Persons (Wales) Measure provides some hope that future Government activity will be framed in this way.

In-work Poverty

With the majority of disadvantaged households with children now having at least one parent in work, there is an urgent need for Government to seek to address in-work poverty. The idea of a living wage has been debated by economists for some time, yet there is now a critical need for employers to be reminded of their responsibility to pay wages that lift employees and their families above the poverty threshold. Presently, the employment market traps many families in poverty (Harker 2006), with the state, through the provision of Child Tax Credits, subsidising low wage rates. Building a new partnership between families, employers and Government would also help to repair the damaging mistrust that presently exists (Hirsch 2008). Further work is therefore required to reach a consensus about what constitutes adequate pay and conditions to free families from poverty to ensure that 'work pays'.

Role of the private sector

Statutory duties have recently been placed on public sector bodies by the Children and Families (Wales) Measure. However, the role and responsibility of the private sector in tackling poverty has not been subject to the same level of scrutiny and debate. Yet the role of the private sector, particularly in relation to the broader well-being dimensions of child poverty, is crucial if the Welsh Assembly Government's ambition is to be met. For example, the need to address poverty of access to play and leisure has been recognised by Government, with recent evidence given to the National Assembly for Wales Children and Young People Committee's inquiry into play highlighting the barriers many families face in accessing play and leisure opportunities e.g. due to cost. Many children living in low-income households find that they are excluded from leisure pursuits that many of their peers take for granted. If poverty of play and leisure is to be truly addressed, the role of the private sector is a critical part of this debate. Equally, in relation to the transport agenda, accessibility and cost of public transport has routinely been identified as a key barrier for children and young people seeking to engage in education, training or simply to see friends and take part in activities. Again, it is the private sector which is the largest provider in many areas.

Benefits and tax credits

The UK Government has a key role in providing an income 'safety net' through benefits for those who are unable to work e.g. due to ill-health or unemployment. Key out-of-work benefits, such as Job Seekers' Allowance

(JSA), have not kept pace with salaries and are not worth the same now in real terms as they were in the late 1990s. As McCormick and Harrop (2010) have pointed out, decisions on taxes and benefits are made by the UK Government without much reference to the devolved administrations. It is essential that the Welsh Assembly Government is involved in the discussions about policy on reserved matters. There are encouraging signs that this is changing with improved engagement between lead officials in each nation. We also believe that benefits should be increased to lift families above the poverty threshold and take-up campaigns should be improved to ensure that households are receiving all their entitlements.

Immediate future

There is presently real anxiety and apprehension amongst lobbyists, political commentators, children's sector organisations and many Welsh Ministers and service providers over what the immediate future holds, given cuts in public spending. Speculation about heavy job losses, public sector cuts, a reduction in welfare spending and the impact of the spending review on the Welsh Assembly Government's budget does not leave those concerned with child poverty with much optimism in relation to the drive to tackle child poverty. Many of the existing programmes and services rely heavily on national and local government funding, and cuts in spending will threaten the foundations on which progress has been over recent years.

> **There is presently real anxiety and apprehension... over what the immediate future holds**

Whilst the services that disadvantaged families and communities rely on in their day-to-day lives are under threat, the lives of the most vulnerable families are being changed in other ways too. The Institute for Fiscal Studies analyses of the recent budget and Comprehensive Spending Review provided independent evidence that political decisions had hit the poorest most. Without an impact assessment being made of the consequences of further cuts in Government spending and services, there is a real fear that actions will disproportionately impact on the vulnerable and low paid most.

Against this backdrop, the UK Government is continuing to emphasise that the route out of poverty is through work, with greater emphasis on lone parents seeking employment, reassessments of long-term benefit recipients alongside harsher sanctions for those who fail to comply. This despite evidence that employment opportunities in many parts of Wales are in short supply, with public transport and childcare provision also proving inadequate. Though work remains important in the fight to eradicate child poverty, there needs to be a greater recognition that other action needs to take place alongside this priority, and that welfare-to-work programmes are adapted to the specific circumstances and challenges in Wales.

The will to do something surely remains. Following a successful European Year and the recent adoption of a European target to reduce child poverty levels across all EU states (Eurochild 2010), now is the time for the Welsh

Assembly Government to truly stand proud, show leadership and strength by demonstrating that social policy can be done very differently here in Wales. Whether the way to do something will be frustrated in the coming months and years from the current economic turmoil and an ever-shrinking budget remains of course to be seen.

Sean O'Neill
is Policy Director,
Children in Wales.
The views in this article
are not necessarily those
of Children in Wales.

References   Centre for the Analysis of Social Exclusion (2010) *An Anatomy of Economic Inequality in the UK: Report of the National Equality Panel,* CASE: London

Consumer Focus Wales (2010) *Consumer Finances in Wales: Debt and Credit Use,* CFW: Cardiff

End Child Poverty Network Cymru (2006) *Tackling Child Poverty in Wales: A Good Practice Guide for Schools,* Children in Wales: Cardiff

Eurochild (2010) *Europe 2020 and the European Platform against Poverty: Briefing Paper 07,* Eurochild: Brussels

Frazer, H., Marlier, E. and Nicaise (2010) *A Social Inclusion Roadmap for Europe,* Garant: Antwerp

Hanley, T. (2009) *Engaging Public Support for Eradicating Child Poverty,* Joseph Rowntree Foundation: York

Harker, L. (2006) *Delivering on Child Poverty: What would it Take?* DWP: London

Hirsch, D. (2008) *What is Needed to End Child Poverty in 2020?,* Joseph Rowntree Foundation: York

Joseph Rowntree Foundation (2008) *A Minimum Income Standard for Britain: What People Think,* JRF: York

McCormick, J. and Harrop, A. (2010) *Devolution's Impact on Low-Income People and Places,* JRF: York

Welsh Assembly Government (2008) *Written Statement by Brian Gibbons, Minister for Social Justice and Local Government,* WAG: Cardiff

Waldfogel, J. (2010) *Britain's War on Poverty,* Sage: London

Inspiring **change**

Amy's story

As part of the European Year for Combating Poverty and Social Exclusion Save the Children is running 'Inspiring Change,' a UK-wide programme that supports children and young people to run 'change' projects for the benefit of their communities and, through their involvement, to build their confidence and learn new skills. Over 300 children, young people and their families are directly involved in the activities in the UK giving them the opportunity to tackle poverty in their local area, transforming their own lives and those of others. 'Inspiring Change' gives young people the opportunity to raise awareness of issues that concern them in their community and supports them to develop effective and practical local actions.

The children and young people that we aim to work with are from communities where engagement in this type of project can be difficult. Involvement in an 'Inspiring Change' group can quickly become a positive part of a young person's life and make a significant contribution in increasing confidence, wellbeing, outlook and ambition. There is a strong focus within the groups on both building aspirations and realising the potential for children and young people to have a real say in what happens within the community.

Inspiring Change projects are as diverse as the children and young people involved in the work as they make the decisions about what the focus of the project should be and drive its development.

"Amy has been out of school for approximately four years, during that time both her parents have been seriously ill. Her dad is unable to work and her mum is unsuccessful in trying to find work due to her ill health. Amy has three older sisters, two of whom are single parents. The family are very close but struggle from day to day to find money for basic essentials. Amy worries about her parents' health and the strain that they are under. She worries when people come to the house demanding money for

debts. She feels very isolated and wants to do something to help her family and her community. Through being involved with Inspiring Change she hopes to make a real difference to her area, she wants to help others and try to make life a little bit easier for people in her community.

The family struggle in the area that they live in, their cars have been vandalised, windows have been smashed and family members have been threatened:

> "The physical environment is really important as it affects how you feel. Just as every individual is different our views are based on our experiences. However this is about our lives so it is really important to get it right and to listen to what we have to say."

Amy is a very bright young person and has many aspirations and hopes for the future, but her confidence can easily be knocked. After years of bullying at school and experiencing the difficulties that her family were going through Amy lost all hope:

> "It was like a big dark cloud hanging over my head, I was so depressed, I couldn't do anything, I remember standing on a car park roof and imagining what it would be like to jump off and die."

Amy stopped going to school due to bullying and became very isolated. Services that got involved with the family added to her stress and frustration and fears of the unknown:

I just need somebody to listen and to help

> "People asking the same questions over and over again. 95 per cent of the time it feels like they don't even care. I know what needs to change and what would make things better, I just need somebody to listen and to help."

Amy strongly believes that:

> "The young person knows what they need help with and what they need to be changed, people need to listen."

Amy's family is very closely knit which is something that Amy clearly values, however she can see the bigger picture:

> "I am 16 years old. I have lived in the same place all my life. I have always called this place home."

> "A home is a place where you're loved, you have a stable place

to be that doesn't change, you're more likely to get over mental illnesses when you have people that love you and you have that love and security around you."

Amy has battled with depression over many years but is now at a point where she can leave the house and take part in group activities. Amy is due to start college in September but worries about being able to travel there, being able to buy books and equipment and in having space and time to get her homework done. She recognises what an opportunity this is for her and is determined to be successful as she sees it as a key to being able to make life better for her and her family. Amy still has lessons to learn and has been bruised by bad experiences in the past, she worries about what people think of her, but at the same time is determined to create a strong and confident image and to express her views on what mental health issues and dealing with poverty can be like to contend with.

> people like me don't often get opportunities like this

Through her involvement with Inspiring Change, Amy has spoken out at key events to represent the voice of young people who do not get the opportunity to speak out and has also been involved in the staff recruitment process at Save the Children. Amy has blossomed in these roles and has made amazing progress just by being asked her opinion and being listed to.

"The fact that people like me don't often get opportunities like this is important for people to realise. In so many ways I am grateful to Save the Children for giving me the chance to do things that otherwise I wouldn't have been able to do. Other children and young people in similar situations to me could end up on the streets or even dead because they haven't been given the chances that I have had. You get the chance to build friendships with people who you wouldn't have ever met if you hadn't got involved with Save the Children."

Amy is a pseudonym.
Compiled by Save the Children.

Work, worklessness and poverty amongst adults in Wales

Victoria Winckler

THE QUESTION OF POVERTY amongst working age adults has received less attention than either child poverty or poverty amongst older people. This lack of attention is surprising because it is parents' low incomes that are the root cause of child poverty, whilst poverty in retirement is associated with a low income during working life. The lack of attention is also surprising because the poverty amongst those of working age in Wales has proved to be much more resistant to change than that amongst older people and children.

This chapter looks at the poverty amongst people of working age in Wales today. It argues that a great deal of the incidence of low income today can be linked with changes in the economy and labour market over the last thirty years, the effects of which have been to entrench low pay and low incomes into the structure of Wales's labour market. This, together with the prospects for the economy over the next five years, makes the outlook for eradicating poverty challenging indeed.

> a great deal of the incidence of low income today can be linked with changes in the economy and labour market over the last thirty years

Working age poverty in Wales

Whilst many people with an interest in poverty issues can readily quote the proportion of children living in poverty in Wales, the proportion of working age adults in poverty comes less readily to mind. Yet the figures are no less shocking – in 2008/09, just over a fifth of the population of working age (22 per cent to be precise) lived in households with an income of less than 60 per cent of the median for their household type, after housing costs. They number about 350,000 people.[1] Although Wales has by no means the highest rates of working age poverty in the UK, with London, the North East and North West of England and the West Midlands all having higher rates, Wales's rate was nevertheless higher than the UK average and higher too than Scotland, Northern Ireland and England.

The greatest risk of being in poverty occurs amongst working-age people in unemployed households, with 70 per cent of them having a low income. The risk is only slightly smaller, at just under 60 per cent, for people in households where all adults are economically inactive.[2] The high risk of poverty for these unemployed and other workless households is closely associated with benefit levels which are in most cases simply not enough to lift them above the relevant poverty threshold.

Working greatly reduces the chances of living in poverty, but, importantly, does not eliminate it. Only for people in households where all adults have some paid work is the risk of poverty very low (5 per cent) – for people in households where only one adult works (or where only part-time work is done in a single adult household) the poverty rate is 28 per cent.[3]

Wales's 350,000 working-age poor are, then, split roughly equally between those in workless households (53 per cent) and those in working households (47 per cent). It is worth looking at each of these groups in more detail.

Worklessness and Poverty

As seen above, there is a very strong association between not working and living on a low income. Whether caused by unemployment, being a lone parent or ill health, the risks of living in poverty for each of these groups of people are over 50 per cent.

Wales has the second highest rate of workless households in the UK, at 16.9 per cent. In April – June 2010, there were 226,000 households, housing 319,000 people, in Wales that did not include any one who was working.[4] Only a fifth of workless households are single adults with children and only a tenth are couple households with children.[5]

The proportion of workless households (and the number of people living in them) in Wales has proved stubbornly resistant to change. It increased slightly between 1997 and 2001, then gradually fell to a low of 14.7 per cent in 2007.[6] The proportion has since risen again and now exceeds the 1997 rate, the progress of the early years of the century undone in just two years.

The association between worklessness and poverty is because worklessness, apart for a few lucky winners of the lottery or inheritors of family fortunes, means people are dependent on benefits for their income. In 2010, nearly one in five of the population of working age in Wales claimed an out-of-work benefit, a total of 366,510 people. About half of these claimed Incapacity Benefit, and a further fifth claimed Job Seekers' Allowance. More than half of claimants in 2010 are under the age of 45.[7] Claimants are able to receive several different benefits depending on their circumstances, as well as benefits in kind such as free school meals. Nevertheless, for most claimants and households benefits are very modest: the headline rate of Job Seekers' Allowance (JSA) for those with sufficient National Insurance contributions was £65.45 a week. Income-based JSA, which takes into account other sources of household income, was a *maximum* of £65.45 for a single person and a *maximum* of £102.75 for a couple. With these levels of benefit, it is hardly surprising that poverty and worklessness are so closely linked.

Whilst the relationship between worklessness and poverty is, then, fairly obvious, it is less clear why Wales has such a high proportion of workless households. To consider this, we need to turn to Wales's recent economic and labour market history.

Worklessness and shifts in employment

Wales in the 1970s was very different from today.[8] In 1974, there were a total of 992,000 people in work, about four out of ten of them women. For men, engineering, transport and labouring were key occupations: these three occupational groups accounted for a third of men's jobs, with mining, quarrying and agriculture accounting for a further ten per cent. Women, in contrast, tended to work in service, clerical and sales occupations. Unemployment in 1974 stood at just 33,400 people.

In just five years, between 1979 and 1984, one in seven of Wales's jobs disappeared

Employment grew throughout the 1970s, with the numbers of employees reaching over a million people (1,033,000) in 1979. Alongside this was, however, an increase in unemployment, which more than doubled between 1974 and 1979. But this was nothing compared with what was to come.

After 1979, Wales's fortunes then changed dramatically. In just five years, between 1979 and 1984, one in seven of Wales's jobs disappeared. Men were particularly hard hit losing a fifth of their jobs during this period. Factory after factory across Wales shed hundreds of workers or closed down altogether, taking with them the cornerstone of many local economies. In the mid 1980s, colliery closures began to take effect as well. Hardly surprisingly in these bleak times, unemployment in Wales rocketed to 168,000 by 1986, with male unemployment hitting around 16 per cent.

Wales's traditional industrial communities were without doubt hardest hit by that recession. More than a third of manufacturing jobs disappeared in just five years, as did about a quarter of jobs in energy and water industries. Total unemployment hit nearly 17 per cent in Mid Glamorgan and West Glamorgan in 1985, and was even higher for males in valleys communities.

Although there has been some recovery from these blows, it has been extremely slow. Overall, employment gradually increased, albeit with a few blips on the way, but it would be 18 years before employment was restored to 1979 levels.[9] However, and this is an extremely important point, male employment has **never** recovered: the decline begun in the early 1980s continued throughout the 1990s, reversing for a brief period between 1999 and 2007, and then resumed. By 2010 there were 83,000 fewer men in employment than there were in 1979 – a 13 per cent decline in thirty years.

These changes in headline figures conceal much more complex shifts in the make-up of the economy and labour market. Crucially, many of the occupations that men worked in have all but disappeared. Mining and quarrying, which in 1971 employed 36,000 – 5 per cent of all employed men – has vanished as both a statistical category and an occupation. The other staples of the male working world, engineering, transport and labouring, have also shrunk dramatically. In contrast, the numbers of various professional and managerial occupations have soared: in 1981 barely one in four men worked in professional and managerial jobs, but by 2009 the proportion was more than four out of ten.

The shifts in the occupational mix compounded the decline in total male employment. What they meant in practice was that, for men unable to make the transition from miner to manager or from transport operative to technician, the prospects were even bleaker than the overall contraction in male employment suggests.

So where did the men displaced from the labour market go? Some of course moved away from Wales altogether, getting on their bikes to find work in England or abroad.[10] Others set up their own businesses, as the many stories about steelworkers turned cake decorators or miners turned social workers attest. But the vast majority seem to have left the labour market altogether. Some re-appeared in the unemployment statistics of the time, either as long-term claimants or cycling in and out of periods of work and unemployment. That male unemployment in Wales remained above 1979 levels for more than twenty years, notwithstanding the many schemes to tackle it, is the clearest possible evidence of this.

But others disappeared into 'economic inactivity', a statistical catch-all that covers everyone from the terminally ill, to the prematurely retired to students to stay-at-home mothers and, crucially, those who Beatty and Fothergill[11] call the 'hidden unemployed". In 1984, 16.6 per cent of working age males were economically inactive. The rate gradually rose over the next twenty years to 23 per cent in 2001 as thousands of men became 'inactive', many of them receiving Incapacity Benefit. Today, it is still clear that 'inactivity' includes a substantial proportion of people who would like to work – in 2009/10 more than a quarter of 'economically inactive' men said they want a job.[12]

Of course the processes that underlie this shift from work to worklessness are a good deal more complex than a simple one-way transfer from job to unemployment to Incapacity Benefit – although there is some evidence that this *did* happen to some men, particularly in the south Wales coalfield, as a result of government efforts to reduce the headline unemployment figures.[13] Lack of prospects for young men looking for work for the first time is also a significant factor, as are high levels of ill-health and disability in many parts of Wales.

working-age poverty in Wales today has some of its origins in the massive restructuring of the economy that took place in the 1980s and 1990s

To sum up this section, working-age poverty in Wales today has some of its origins in the massive restructuring of the economy that took place in the 1980s and 1990s. It took nearly 20 years to remedy the massive shake-out of jobs that took place during that time, and for men that recovery has yet to take place. The loss of jobs inevitably resulted in higher unemployment and higher levels of economic inactivity, both of which carry high risks of poverty. Whilst people in workless, low-income households in 2010 are not necessarily the same people who lost their jobs thirty years previously (although some undoubtedly are), they are nevertheless living with the consequences of the withdrawal of thousands of jobs from the labour market and the absence of replacements.

The new poor? Working households on low incomes

The restructuring of the economy also offers us a way of understanding poverty amongst households where at least one adult is working – those in 'in-work' poverty – although it owes less to the legacy of the 1980s and more to recent notions of 'flexible working'.

In 2006/07-2008/09, nearly half (47 per cent) of working age people in poverty lived in a household where at least one person did some form of paid work. At least some of the explanation for this phenomenon seems to lie in the relatively low proportion of people in households where all adults work. This type of household has a small risk of poverty (at just 5 per cent), and so it follows that the higher the proportion of 'all-working' households the lower the likelihood of poverty. In Wales, a slightly lower proportion of people live in 'all-working' households than in most other parts of the UK. At 48 per cent, only Northern Ireland and London have lower rates whilst the North East of the England has the same rate.[14]

The obverse of this is that Wales has a slightly higher proportion of adults in households where one adult is workless (a part-working household) than other parts of the UK, although the difference between Wales and other nations and regions is mostly not particularly large. Being in a part-working household carries a higher risk of poverty than all-working households, at 28 per cent.

So although some of the explanation for Wales's high levels of in-work poverty lies in how 'work-rich' a household does, it is by no means a sufficient explanation. There is another factor – pay.

The relationship between low pay for individuals and low income for households is not direct: a low-paid person may live in a household with a high-paid person, and thus have a high household income. Work undertaken by the Bevan Foundation and the New Policy Institute in 2006[15] estimated that although about 65 per cent of low-income households comprised low-paid workers, only about a quarter of low-paid workers lived in low-income households.

Two issues drive whether a low-paid worker is in a low-income household. First, hours of work are critical to the income of a low-paid household. At the time of writing the report, it was feasible for a household whose members were all low paid (at National Minimum Wage rates) to avoid poverty if all of them worked 30 hours a week or more. However if one or more in the household worked fewer hours than this, i.e. worked part-time or not at all, then the risks of poverty increased.

Yet the trend in the labour market has been very much away from full-

"

In terms of earnings, the most poorly-paid 20 per cent of full-time workers earn less than £301 a week

time work.[16] In Wales part-time working rose by 15 per cent between 2004 and 2010, notwithstanding the recession, and now accounts for a quarter of all employment. The proportion of women who work part-time is even higher at 43 per cent, while for men the proportion is a lower, but nevertheless historic high, of around 16 per cent. In contrast, between 2004 and 2010 there was a net decrease in full-time working, which fell by 43,000. The decrease for male full-timers over this period was even greater. Within the shift to part-time working is also a shift to so-called flexible working – variable hours contracts (including zero hours contracts), temporary working and commission-only arrangements.

Of course not everyone is able to work full-time even if jobs are available. Caring for children or for adult relatives may make working more than 30 hours a week impossible or, with the costs of alternative care far exceeding the earning capacity of low-paid workers, unaffordable. For these people, part-time working is a means of combining home responsibilities with work.

So, whilst full-time work has the best prospects for lifting a household out of poverty the number of full-time jobs is declining. Moreover not everyone is able to work full-time, even if a job was available. Part-time work, which offers at best mixed prospects of a route out of poverty, is, on the other hand, growing. The changing pattern of employment seems, then, to be a factor in in-work poverty.

The second driver of poverty in working households is low pay. Two thirds of low-income households comprise low-paid workers, and for them the hourly rate of pay is critical. Defining low pay as £7 an hour, one in eight male full-time workers and one in six female full-time workers in Wales in 2009 were low paid.[17] In terms of earnings, the most poorly-paid 20 per cent of full-time workers earn less than £301 a week.[18]

Whether or not low-paid workers live in poor households depends on a number of factors, including the number of hours they work, the type of household they live in, whether other household members are working, and their housing costs. The struggle to avoid poverty is clear if we look at the lowest paid 20 per cent of full-timers.[19] Their £301 per week gross translates into take-home pay of approximately £244 a week (using 2009/10 tax and national insurance deduction tables).[20] Whilst this sum would be enough to lift a single person out of poverty (for which an income before housing costs of £164 per week is required) it is not enough to lift a couple without dependent children (for whom the before housing cost income required to escape poverty is £244 a week). For a couple household with dependent children, Child Benefit and Child Tax Credit raise household income to just on the poverty threshold before housing costs.

The challenge of earning enough to avoid poverty is even greater for part-timers. Amongst this group, about 43 per cent of both male and female part-time workers earn £7 an hour or less. The combination of fewer hours and low pay is constrains part-time workers' earnings very substantially. In 2009, the median gross weekly wage of part-timers in 2009 was just £151.70,[21] not enough to lift *any* household type above the poverty threshold unless they have zero housing costs and / or substantial additional income from earnings by other household members, benefits or tax credits. Indeed, apart from some exceptions where income is topped up by tax credits, it only makes economic sense for an individual to work at the median part-time wage if other household members are working.

Changes in the labour market have thus impacted on in-work poverty in two key ways. First the decline in full-time employment and increase in part-time working impact on *total* earnings, simply because fewer hours are worked. Second, the shift to part-time working also means there are more jobs paying low hourly rates in the economy. These together significantly increase the likelihood of living in in-work poverty.

Conclusion

Working-age poverty in Wales is very clearly associated with the deep-seated and long-term shifts that have taken place in the economy and labour market. These changes are continuing apace. Economic restructuring in the 1980s and 1990s saw massive job loss, which particularly affected men. Not only did the sheer number of jobs not recover for nearly two decades, but during the recovery the nature of jobs shifted towards service sector jobs and part-time working. Those who could not get work as a result of these changes have ended up in workless households, dependent on benefits and at very high risk of poverty.

Those jobs that remain in the economy are changing rapidly too. The continuing decline in full-time work and increase in part-time work bring a risk of low hourly pay and low gross weekly earnings. To get a job in Wales in 2010 is most definitely not a guaranteed route out of poverty.

The outlook over the next five years is very uncertain. Workless households, living on benefit, face cuts in their income unless they are deemed 'severely disabled'. Changes to Housing Benefit, Council Tax Benefit, Working Tax Credit and Child Benefit, together with means-testing of Incapacity Benefit could have a substantial cumulative impact on benefit recipients. It seems inevitable that workless households who are already on a low income will be driven even deeper into poverty unless they are able to find work.

Even if the UK economy does recover, itself an uncertain prospect, it is far from clear if Wales will enjoy the benefits of that growth. Indeed, Wales's dependence on the public sector and the forecasts of job losses from spending cuts make the prospects of increases in employment in the short term seem remote. If and when growth in total employment does eventually occur, it is likely that the decline of full-time work and growth of

> **The continuing decline in full-time work and increase in part-time work bring a risk of low hourly pay and low gross weekly earnings. To get a job in Wales in 2010 is most definitely not a guaranteed route out of poverty**

part-time work will continue. Add to this probably downward pressure on wages and on conditions too, and there seems to be little prospect of work providing a route out of poverty for thousands of people of working age in Wales.

Victoria Winckler
is Director of
the Bevan
Foundation

Notes

1 Department for Work and Pensions (2010) *Households Below Average Income: An analysis of the income distribution income distribution* 1994/95 – 2008/09. London: DWP
2 www.poverty.org.uk
3 www.poverty.org.uk
4 Office for National Statistics (2010) Work and Worklessness among households, Table 1(iii) and Table 2(iii). Available at http://www.statistics.gov.uk/statbase/Product.asp?vlnk=8552
5 http://www.poverty.org.uk/w50/index.shtml
6 Office for National Statistics (2010) op. cit.
7 Office for National Statistics, Benefit Claimants, via NOMIS, 4th Nov. 2010
8 All the statistics in this section are derived from Welsh Assembly Government (1998) *Digest of Welsh Statistics* vol. 2, 1974 – 1996, Chapter 7.
9 Annual Population Survey 2010, via Nomis, 4th November 2010
10 Beatty, C. and Fothergill, S. (2005) The diversion from 'unemployment' to 'sickness' across British regions and districts. *Regional Studies*, 39, pp. 837-854.
11 Beatty, C. and Fothergill, S., and Powell, R. (2006) Twenty years on: has the economy of the UK coalfields recovered. *Environment and Planning A*, 39, pp. 1654-1675.
12 Annual Population Survey (2010) via NOMIS, 4th Nov. 2010
13 Beatty, C. and Fothergill, S. (2005), op. cit.
14 Office for National Statistics (2010) op. cit.
15 Bevan Foundation and New Policy Institute (2006) *Dreaming of £250 a week*. Tredegar: Bevan Foundation
16 The statistics in the rest of this section are from the Annual Population Survey, via NOMIS.
17 www.poverty.org.uk
18 Welsh Assembly Government (2009) *Annual Survey of Hours and Earnings,* 2009. Statistical Bulletin SB78/2009.
19 Ibid.
20 In addition, council tax ought to be deducted to be directly comparable with the before housing cost poverty threshold.
21 Annual Survey of Hours and Earnings, 2009, NOMIS

Poverty and social exclusion?
No, I was just doing my best to get by

Jane's story

When we consider the concept of poverty and social exclusion, many think of extreme deprivation, homelessness and starvation. However, this is not always the case. Lots of us will know someone who has or is experiencing poverty on some level and not even be aware of it themselves. Many people who have experienced forms or poverty or social exclusion do not identify themselves under those headings but instead feel that they were just trying to get by, or make ends meet.

Here is the story of Jane Williams who has worked for the NHS for 31 years as a nurse. Jane is married to John and has three children aged 28, 25 and 15. Jane separated from her first husband when her eldest children, Louise and Marie, were 6 and 3 years old.

❝ We had been living in Yorkshire, but I decided it was best for me and the girls if we returned to Bridgend as I knew the area and had family and friends there too.

It was a huge adjustment for us all. The girls' father remained in Yorkshire, so suddenly I was doing everything more or less on my own. I had to work full-time as I needed to have an income to look after the girls, but that presented its own problems. Working full-time shift work and looking after two young children was definitely a challenge. I was fortunate that their Grandparents helped out when they could, but a fair amount of my income had to go on childcare.

Plus at least half of my salary went on the mortgage and that was before bills were paid – it was the '80s recession and times were tough then. I was very proud though, and tried my hardest to make sure I didn't get into debt.

I don't remember going cold in the house, but I remember food wasn't always a priority for me – especially just before payday. Making sure there was enough food for the girls was my main goal and they ate an awful lot of boiled potatoes during those years. There were certainly no luxuries at that time and, looking back, I'm glad that branded clothes and fashion weren't as important as they are now, so I wasn't under pressure from the girls for trendy new clothes. They tended to get new clothes at Christmas time and birthdays, but not a lot else throughout the rest of the year.

I remember feeling quite lonely at times. It was just the girls and me in the house and they were in bed early in the evening so I spent quite a lot of time alone. Many of my friends were either without kids and had a lot of independence or were married so were spending time with their families, so I didn't have many visitors. I couldn't afford much of a social life really and at times I found that difficult. Plus if I ever did manage some time out, I would feel guilty that I should have spent that money on the girls. That feeling of guilt lasted a long time actually – even now I prefer to buy for other people than for myself.

Even though things were a struggle, I do look back at that period with a smile on my face. We had some really good times and it didn't revolve around money – we made our own fun. I think we need to remind ourselves of that a little more. We spent a lot of time outdoors and going to things that were free. One of my fondest memories is reading to Louise and Marie at the top of the stairs before they went to bed. We all enjoyed that time together and it didn't cost a penny.

> I feel very proud of us and what we achieved.

I feel very proud of us and what we achieved. Ultimately, I wouldn't be who I am now if I hadn't have gone through that time. I met my husband John in 1990 and we have our youngest daughter Rose. I feel blessed with what I have and I definitely appreciate things a lot more having gone through that experience.

When we first started talking about this article on poverty and social exclusion, I couldn't see how it related to me. As far as I was, and still am concerned really, I didn't suffer from poverty and social exclusion, I was just trying to do my best for my children and get by as well as I could. But when I look back now I can acknowledge that it was a difficult time, that I did have to make sacrifices and I can't believe there were times that I had to go without food so that the kids could eat – so on some level I suppose I was pretty hard-up.

The sad thing I've come to realise is that there are so many people in Wales that will have been in very similar and often worse situations than myself. I think that's one of the reasons that I'll always work for the NHS – it's so important for everyone, regardless of how much money they have, to have access to healthcare.

My story is a happy one – we overcame our difficulties and made a better life for ourselves, and I don't take that for granted. Sadly this isn't the case for many others though and we need to make sure that adequate support is there for all the other families that are still having tough times, especially as things look as though they may get a lot worse in the coming years.

Compiled by Amber Courtney, UNISON

I took **the job**

Sian's story _____

"I'm 32 years old and I live on my own with my three children, all in primary school. I don't live with the children's father, although they do see him a lot, he doesn't give us any money because he's got too many debts of his own. I grew up in a small village in Wales, speaking Welsh at home and at school. My English is OK, but I feel stupid speaking it to strangers and my Welsh isn't posh enough to get a good job.

I grew up with an older sister and two younger ones. My dad died when I was young and me and my older sister ended up doing the cooking and looking after the house and just taking care of the other two, especially 'cos my youngest sister has a learning disability. She lives with me now and is at college. I try to make sure she's ok. My mum always worked – two jobs at least – she always paid the bills and she was always knackered. She died four years ago, it took me six months to leave the house. I don't really have any support now, except my best friend. One sister married and moved away – her husband's an engineer. She did really well, got their own house and everything. The other has a nasty partner, isn't allowed to go anywhere.

I want my kids to do better than I did at school, I want them to get a good job and have proper qualifications. I don't want them struggling to pay their rent and their bills. I'd really like them to have music lessons and swimming lessons and go on the school holidays, go for sleepovers, and drive to the cinema and then Pizza Hut, all the stuff we didn't do. They're doing ok at school, come home with stars and badges. My eldest though, he had quite a few yellow cards last year – he's no angel but sometimes I think they get a picture of a child in their head and then that's it until they leave primary school and by then it's just stuck and he's stuck. I try to keep talking to the teachers, so that they know I want them to do well…. I worry too that I won't be able to help them enough, I don't have GCSEs, I don't know many people who I could ask to help and we don't have a computer. I really want them to do better than me, but it's a

> I worry too that I won't be able to help them enough, I don't have GCSEs

lot for them to do on their own.

I've been volunteering for the last three years at a local community centre, four mornings a week, I do some administration, booking rooms, answering the phone, writing letters, organising things, taking minutes, doing the post and the petty cash. Sometimes I end up helping out at the crèche, in the kitchen or the community garden, there's not much I won't do. To be honest, I started 'cos I thought I might get a job, I want my kids to see me working, I want to give them more. In some ways the volunteering has saved me, it got me out of the house at a time when I didn't know how I was going to carry on, I knew if I went to the doctor she'd give me anti-depressants and I didn't want that. I didn't want to not miss my mum.

I've done lots of training courses, more than I ever did at school – confidence building, Nordic walking, wreath-making, community development, childcare, assertiveness, mentoring, oh loads of stuff, I've got so many OCN certificates, you'd think I was a genius.

I've learnt useful stuff too, stuff that no-one tells you. You can get money to pay for courses and childcare, one agency will pay for driving lessons and interview clothes, there's help if you want to do childcare at home. And if you've got problems, there are organisations that understand how to help you, it's amazing really.

The centre persuaded me to do a proper admin course at the college – you get a level 3 qualification at the end, and lots of skills. I'm really excited and I'm really enjoying it. The Welsh is hard, but I work on the file every day. The Job Centre Plus don't like it though, they send me for shit jobs, cleaning, care work, bar work, shop work, 20 miles away, all work I can't do for different reasons. They don't care about the course, and I have to go to the things they want me to go to or they say they'll stop my money. I wish they'd listen and work with me, it feels like fighting them all the time. Although one woman was great, she said I'd be better going to my course than doing interview skills with her 'cos I'd already done it.

> **I wish they'd listen and work with me, it feels like fighting them all the time**

Before the summer holidays I was offered an admin job at the centre. I cried and that's not like me. Couldn't believe they'd want me, couldn't believe they'd think that I could do the job, just amazing, unbelievable. I went to the Job Centre to work out the money, and the man said that I'd lose the carers allowance and I'd be thirty pounds worse off. He didn't say 'don't take it', but he wasn't encouraging me either. I wanted him to make me feel that it'd be ok if I didn't take it and it'd be ok if I took it, whatever happened he'd help me sort it out, but he wasn't like that, he just said this is the money, it's up to you. It took me ages to decide, what if I couldn't do the job, what if I couldn't leave the house again, what if I couldn't manage on the money, what if the job ends with the cuts, just so many things. My head was spinning. I didn't know what to do. I wanted to talk to my mum.

I took the job, I start in September.

Sian is a pseudonym.
Compiled by Oxfam Cymru

Older people and poverty in Wales

Graeme Francis

WALES HAS THE HIGHEST PROPORTION of people of pensionable age and the highest proportion of people over 80 in the UK.[1] All older people should enjoy an adequate standard of living and a level of income which enables them to live comfortably, and no one should have to endure a calamitous reduction in their standard of living when they retire. Yet, despite progress over the last decade, poverty remains a serious issue for many older people with 119,000 older people in Wales, and 2 million older people in the UK as a whole, estimated to be living in a house-hold with an income below the recognised relative poverty threshold.[2]

> **poverty remains a serious issue for many older people**

Evidence is mixed about how poverty levels amongst older people have changed over recent years. According to figures from the Department for Work and Pensions (DWP), 26 per cent of people of pensionable age in Wales were in low income households in 1996/97 compared to 18 per cent in 2008/09, though the fall in Wales was smaller than across the rest of the UK. These figures match the general trend across the whole population over the same time period. However, the figures for older people differ depending on whether their income is measured before or after an allowance for housing costs. No consistent trend emerges using figures before housing costs, but the proportion in poverty decreases using after housing costs figures. In 2008/09 pensioners were more likely to be in the second lowest income quintile and less likely to be in the top two quintiles of the income distribution than the population as a whole.[3] Between 13 and 15 per cent of older people were in persistent poverty (being on a low income for three years out of four) between 2002 and 2005, 1.5 to 2.5 times more likely than amongst working-age adults.[4] A higher proportion of pensioners than the population as a whole is poor when income is assessed before housing costs.[5]

Patterns of poverty

Government social policies in recent years, such as the minimum income guarantee in Pension Credit, Winter Fuel Allowance and concessions for things such as local travel and TV licenses, have made a recognisable difference to poverty amongst older people. Despite these initiatives, poverty and social exclusion still remain as significant issues for older people in Wales. Detailed analysis of the figures reveals distinct patterns of poverty amongst older people:

- In general, the older a person is, the greater the likelihood is that they have a low income.[6]
- A higher proportion of single pensioners living alone are in low-income households than any other group in society,[7] and single older people are more likely to be in poverty than couples, irrespective of their age.[8]
- Pensioners living in a household headed by someone from an ethnic minority are more likely to be in a low-income household. This is particularly the case in households headed by someone of Pakistani or Bangladeshi ethnic origin.[9]

Overall, levels of poverty and social exclusion are highest amongst older women living alone.[10]

The causes of poverty are many and complex, but an understanding of the factors which drive people into poverty in later life is essential if we are to use the right methods to tackle the problems. Many older people living in households below the poverty threshold will have been in this situation during their working lives e.g. from prolonged unemployment, social exclusion or the effects of a disability. For these individuals and households, while strategies and support mechanisms for pensioner poverty may help to raise basic income they may not be tackling the causes of their poverty in the first place.

> **understanding of the factors which drive people into poverty in later life is essential**

For others, the ageing process itself may be a contributory factor. Some people experience a disastrous reduction in income when they retire or can no longer find work. This is often as a result of inadequate pension provision, either because they are reliant on the state pension with no additional personal or occupational provision, or because of failures of pension schemes due to changes in financial markets. These issues can be particularly pronounced for women who may have spent long periods of their working lives running households and caring for dependent children and, as a result, are often not entitled to the full state pension.

Bereavement is also sometimes a major factor contributing to poverty, with the loss of a partner (and often a pension income) liable to cause hardship for the surviving partner – for perhaps the first time.

Income in later life

The range of income sources amongst older people reflect individual circumstances, but generally fall into four main categories:
- pensions
- benefits and entitlements
- employment
- income from savings and investments (including potential income in the form of assets such as property).

Older people in poverty generally rely on pensions, benefits and entitlements which are not, on their own, sufficient to protect them from hardship or to raise people above the poverty threshold.

The state pension and retirement ages have been areas of considerable discussion and debate in recent times. Demographic trends have resulted in an increase in the number of people in retirement whilst at the same time a lower birth-rate in recent decades has led to fewer people of working age. The net effect is a widely predicted crisis in state and private pensions as too few people pay income tax and National Insurance contributions to support state pensions and the costs of age-related public services. The most recent study however indicates that previous predictions may have overstated the costs of increased longevity as they did not fully take account of associated improvements in health and independence which will mean that age-related demands on pensions and health and care services are deferred until later in life.[11]

As life expectancy in the UK increases a corresponding increase in the state pension age is inevitable. The current Conservative-Liberal Democrat Coalition Government has announced that men and women's pension ages will be equalised at 65 in 2018 and rise to 66 in 2020. The rise in pension age must however be part of a package of sustainable pension and workplace reform. Longer working lives must be matched with improved attitudes to, and support for, older workers. It will be detrimental to poverty levels if the increase in state pension age is not matched by necessary reform of employment law and practices and improved societal attitudes to working longer. The significant barriers currently faced by people in their 50s and 60s when looking for work or seeking to change job must be addressed as it is clearly in no one's interests to create a new cohort of people dependent on unemployment benefits in their 60s.

In enacting reforms, governments must also recognise that many people stop working in their early 60s for good reasons and not necessarily by choice. In some occupations it is easier to continue working than in others – improved re-training and flexible working opportunities will be necessary to ensure that later eligibility for the state pension does not adversely affect people in demanding manual jobs, for whom longer careers may simply not be an option.

The state pension

The UK Government has restored the link between the state pension and average earnings from April 2011, and has announced a 'triple lock' which will guarantee that the basic state pension will rise by a minimum of 2.5 per cent or in line with earnings or prices, whichever is greater. This is a welcome move which, over the long-term, will help to maintain basic retirement incomes relative to the prosperity of society at large. Earnings inflation is likely to continue to be depressed over the next few years however, which will limit the immediate impact. The level of the state pension (£97.65 per week as of September 2010) is estimated to be one of the lowest in Europe when looked at in comparison to average earnings and it has decreased in its real value continuously since 1980 when the link with earnings was broken. At its peak in 1979 the basic state pension was equivalent to 26 per cent of average earnings,[12] while in 2008 it stood at just 18 per cent.[13] Future guaranteed minimum increases in the state pension are welcome though these alone will not be enough to compensate for the drop in its relative value over the last three decades. In Age Cymru's view, any moves to increase the state pension age should sit alongside work to improve pensioner incomes and reduce poverty. A more generous state pension could be quid pro quo for accelerating the pace at which the state pension age rises. We expect a further UK Government green paper on long-term pension reform to be published by the end of 2010.

Pension Credit was introduced by the UK Government in 2003 as a replacement for other minimum income guarantee benefits. It has two elements: the Guarantee Credit which aims to provide a minimum level of income for older people without additional income as a top-up to the basic state pension; and the Savings Credit which is intended to reward older people with a second pension or modest savings. The current level of the minimum income guarantee under Pension Credit is £132.60 a week (for a single person at the time of writing), above the 60 per cent median household income 'poverty threshold'. Pension Credit has an additional importance because it is a 'passport benefit' which enables those who claim the guaranteed element of the credit to also get help with council tax and housing costs and provides additional support for people who receive Carers Allowance or disability benefits. Unfortunately significant numbers of older people eligible do not claim their entitlement, the reasons for which will be discussed later.

significant numbers of older people eligible do not claim their entitlement

The fact that Pension Credit is required to top-up the state pension for people without other sources of income poses a question about the purpose of the basic state pension. Does it aim to alleviate poverty amongst retired people, as is often assumed; to be a minimum provision for a civilised existence in retirement; or to provide a safety net for those without alternative provision? It appears to be the latter on the basis that Pension Credit is the additional tool to lift people without alternative provision above the poverty threshold. However, given the numbers of people who do not claim Pension Credit, despite being eligible, it is surely right to ask whether we should require people living in poverty to navigate a complex and confusing benefits system to gain access to the 'minimum guaranteed' income our society has deemed they are entitled to? There will always be people who are unable or unwilling to make their own retirement provision and we must be clear about the extent to which state provision intends to protect people from financial hardship or recognised levels of poverty in these situations. Given the number of older people living on incomes below the poverty threshold it must be reasonable to question whether the current system is fit for purpose.

Occupational and private pensions

The UK Government's Pensions Minister, Steve Webb, recently stated that 7 million people across the UK are currently not saving enough to meet their retirement aspirations[14] and over one-third of people in full-time employment are not saving into a non-state pension.[15] In Wales around two-fifths of workers between 30 and 65, and significantly more than half of workers on below-average incomes, do not have a 'current' pension (either an occupational or private pension). The number of workers under 30 with non-state pensions is extremely low.[16]

The last few years have also seen a continuing fall in the numbers of defined-benefit pension schemes open to workers in the private sector and the defined contribution pensions which are replacing them are much more uncertain, as recent economic turmoil has shown. Typical employer contributions are much lower too. In addition, many public sector pension schemes have been eroded in recent years and the spending cuts in forthcoming years will place these under further threat. Recent criticism has focused on the UK Government's announcement that occupational pension payments would in future be linked to the Consumer Price Index (CPI) instead of the Retail Price Index (RPI), which has been used since 1947. The CPI does not include house prices and typically produces a lower measure of inflation, potentially leading to significant reductions in income from existing and future occupational pensions. It has even been claimed that applying these changes retrospectively could risk breaching people's human rights.[17]

To go some way to addressing these issues, auto-enrolment into workplace pensions is scheduled to begin in 2012 following reforms in the Pensions Act 2008. From this date most employees will be automatically enrolled into either their employer's workplace pension or into the National Employment Savings Trust (NEST), a new defined contribution scheme geared towards those with low and moderate earnings. People will be able to choose to opt out, but those who stay will benefit from a compulsory contribution from their employer. However, it is possible that a small minority of people with low and modest earnings, or with interrupted working lives, could be worse-off after making small contributions, so the new system needs to be accompanied by good independent information and guidance to help people make informed decisions. The introduction of auto-enrolment and NEST is an essential move towards universal workplace pension coverage and could in time help to reduce pensioner poverty, though the scheme must be well managed to minimise any negative impact from fluctuations in financial markets.

Other problems with private pensions include annuities and workplace pension schemes that are wound up when the employer goes into liquidation. Most attention has been focused on the need to buy an annuity

> **two-fifths of workers between 30 and 65, and significantly more than half of workers on below-average incomes, do not have a 'current' pension**

at age 75, though this does not affect significant numbers of people. Taxation of annuities impacts upon a greater and increasing number of people who are retiring with one or more small defined contribution pension funds. Due to outdated taxation rules, some people may end up with a 'stranded pot' – a pension fund that is too small to annuitise, that cannot be consolidated with another pension fund, and that cannot be drawn in cash – or only after suffering a high tax deduction. Technical reforms to tax rules and administration could make a real difference to people caught in this situation, while tighter rules on employers' use of pension funds are also needed.

Benefits and entitlements

It has been estimated that poverty among older people could be reduced by a third if there was full take-up of income-related benefits.[18] In Wales 204,000 people currently receive Pension Credit according to figures from the DWP, though it is estimated that about one-third of people eligible do not claim it. In Wales around 90,000 pensioners have no income other than state benefits, which equates to approximately 1 in 5 single older people and 1 in 12 couples.[19]

> **poverty among older people could be reduced by a third if there was full take-up of income-related benefits**

This poses the question of how best to tackle low take-up. The factors which lead to people not claiming their entitlements are numerous and include: lack of information on, or understanding of, the system and what they may be entitled to; a mistaken belief that they would not be eligible for support; a lack of ability or support to correctly complete application processes; and social or personal stigma attached to claiming benefits or 'asking for help'.

Some of these can be addressed, at least in part, by information, advice and support services or by changing some of the language used in this context, for example referring to 'entitlements' as opposed to 'benefits'. However, wholesale change is only likely to result from reform or simplification of the system and automatic payment of benefits. It has long been claimed that simplification of the system through which benefits are administered would lead to improved take-up. The range and diversity of benefits and entitlements in the UK is a result of piecemeal change over decades by different governments seeking to target support at those in most need. However, it ought to be possible to simplify and combine application processes and develop automatic payment mechanisms.

More dramatic progress is only likely if people are paid entitlements automatically. A pilot in England is due to test paying people Pension Credit for a limited period and then inviting them to apply to receive ongoing payments. This intends to re-frame the choice about applying for extra income, applying the 'nudge' lessons of behavioural economics. It is hoped that take-up will significantly increase, both because people often assume they will not be eligible and because they may worry more about losing money they are already receiving than about gaining more. Payments will be made to people who have been identified as likely to be eligible, after matching tax and benefits data. The fact that this can happen at all shows that the mechanisms exist to identify who is eligible for support without complex application procedures. The lessons learned must be used to improve delivery across appropriate schemes.

In addition to Pension Credit and income-based support schemes, 114,700 people over 65 years of age in Wales claim Attendance Allowance to help them cope with the costs of disability, while 97,860 continue to receive Disability Living Allowance for longer-standing conditions for the same purpose.[20] These are vital support mechanisms which help many older people to live independently and to reduce the pressure on NHS and social care services. However both have come under scrutiny in the context of changes to care funding and public spending cuts. It is essential that the central features of these benefits are protected to ensure that older people who are already at an increased risk of poverty are not additionally disproportionately affected by reductions in public spending.

Employment

Paid employment is a major source of income for many older people and, alongside private and occupational pensions, is one of the leading methods of protecting against poverty. Many people continue in employment past state pension age for reasons of choice or necessity, which can be beneficial to the individual themselves and has a clear dividend for society and public finances.

> **Many people continue in employment past state pension age for reasons of choice or necessity**

Since the early 1990s, the number of workers aged over 50 in the UK has risen from 6 million to 8 million over 15 years.[21] However, labour market conditions have worsened significantly over the last 18 months and there is worrying evidence about the impact on older workers. The numbers of people in work between the age of 50 and state pension age in Wales stood at 341,000, or 58.9 per cent of the age group, in July 2010. This was second lowest rate of employment among recognised 'disadvantaged groups', after disabled people. Long-term unemployment is particularly serious amongst older workers (Graph 1): over the past year the number of older job seekers in Wales who have been unemployed for more than 12 months has soared by 67.5 per cent and people in this position now make up 27.3 per cent of all job seekers aged 50 and over.[22] Unfortunately once someone aged over 50 has been out of work for 6-12 months they are unlikely ever to work again.[23] For the country this is a waste of skills, and for the individual it is often devastating in relation to personal finances, health and self-esteem.

Graph 1:

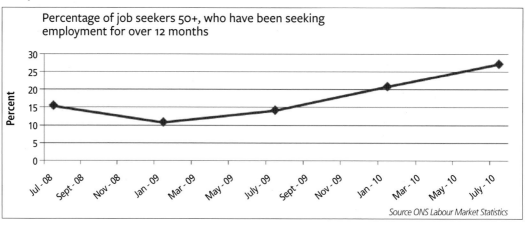

Percentage of job seekers 50+, who have been seeking employment for over 12 months

Source ONS Labour Market Statistics

Providing appropriate counselling and support to help people back into work quickly is essential, but current mechanisms often do not take adequate account of the needs of older people and frequently adopt a 'one size fits all' approach. Research by Age UK shows that older workers believe their knowledge and experience are undervalued, and that they feel pressured to take inappropriate or low-skilled jobs.[24] Crucially, there is a severe lack of suitable retraining opportunities: the bulk of training packages focus on young people with little attention given to older workers wanting (or needing) to change direction or explore a new career.

> **current mechanisms often do not take adequate account of the needs of older people and frequently adopt a 'one size fits all' approach**

Age discrimination in employment remains widespread despite the introduction of the Employment Equality (Age) Regulations in 2006 (which are now absorbed into the Equality Act 2010). 71 per cent of people in Wales indicated that they believed older people were discriminated against on the grounds of their age in employment in a poll for Age Cymru in 2010, while 1 in 5 people (21 per cent) between the ages of 50 and 64 believed they had actively been discriminated against because of their age.[25]

Possibly the clearest example of age discrimination in employment is the Default Retirement Age, which allows employers to force people to retire at age 65. The UK Government has stated its intention to abolish the Default Retirement Age from October 2011. This is a vital step towards limiting some of the most overt discrimination against older workers and is in the interests of both equality and the UK economy. Nevertheless, employers will still need to go further to eliminate discrimination. To retain older workers and fill skills gaps they need to focus on better workplace design, more occupational health support, and greater use of flexible working practices. To achieve this there will need to be much better support and guidance from government and industry bodies.

Savings and investments

Older people who have been able to bring savings, investments or assets into later life have seen the rapid decline of the stock market and cuts in interest rates wipe significant sums off from their retirement incomes. Almost three-quarters of pensioners receive income from savings and while for the majority the amount is small, it can make a useful contribution to annual income. Savings also act as a cushion against unforeseen events, such as care needs or household repairs.

Some older people who have property in retirement may be 'asset-rich, cash-poor'. Their appearance of relative prosperity may mask a struggle to maintain an adequate lifestyle on a low income and an inability to realise the potential of that asset. Medium to large properties may also present real difficulties in terms of modernisation or adequate heating. People who would otherwise have taken the opportunity to downsize or to make use of equity release schemes have been affected by difficult conditions in the housing market.

Financial exclusion

The financial inclusion strategy for Wales identifies older people (and particularly single pensioners) as a group at increased risk of financial exclusion. 5 per cent of households containing people over the age of 85 do not have a bank account,[26] and many older people find it increasingly difficult to access cash free of charge, in particular those with mobility impairments who cannot easily access town centres. Many older people who do have financial products find themselves pushed out of the marketplace by physical barriers such as branch closures, increasing use of new technology, and in some cases outright discrimination.

Being excluded from mainstream financial services means that those who can least afford to do so end up paying more for their basic needs, including the cost of energy (as they cannot benefit from the cheaper tariffs linked to payments by direct debit) and credit (because of a lack of access to affordable rates from mainstream financial services). Exclusion may be exacerbated for some older people because of their specific circumstances, such as difficulties physically accessing banks and building society branches, exclusion from digital technology, and lack of financial capability.

Financial services and government strategies must do more to tackle these issues amongst older people. With more bank branches closing, post offices have the potential to provide a useful access point, especially in rural areas, and the UK Government has prompted debate about expanding the role of the post office in banking, which also has potential for improving the viability of many post office branches. Age Cymru believes that legislation

> **Being excluded from mainstream financial services means that those who can least afford to do so end up paying more for their basic needs**

should be amended to require all banks to provide access via post offices.

The Payments Council has set a target date of 2018 for the end of payment by cheque. Large numbers of older people still rely on personal cheques, and some 21 per cent of consumers say this would cause them a major problem.[27] There is not yet an adequate alternative to cheques and withdrawing them may force some older people to relinquish control of their financial affairs. For example, people with mobility problems may feel that they have no alternative but to give a friend, relative or care worker their cash card and PIN to draw money for them.

Other common concerns around financial services relate to direct or indirect age discrimination. Many of the best deals, and some products in their entirety, are only available online which severely limits their availability to older people. Despite gradual increases in the numbers of older people using online services, 71 per cent of people aged over 65 in the UK had never used the internet in 2008.[28] In insurance services many companies still refuse cover on the grounds of age, preventing people from getting travel or motor insurance. Age UK research in January 2010 revealed that only half of a list of household name insurers would offer cover to mystery shoppers over the age of 80.[29]

There are also indications of rising debt among older people. Average amounts owed by unsecured credit users in their late 50s and early 60s are higher than for any other age group, and although only 25 per cent of households aged 65-74, and 10 per cent aged 75-84 had non-mortgage borrowing, a minority owe very large sums. Recent years also show increases in the number of older people with mortgages. It is difficult to tell whether these trends are a result of specific factors or indicative of longer-term trends and shifts in attitudes. It may be that today's younger generations will bring their spending habits with them into later life, creating a previously unseen level of debt amongst older people.

> **The consequences of living in poverty for older people include loss of independence, difficulty accessing transport, and inability to afford basic essentials**

Conclusion

The consequences of living in poverty for older people include loss of independence, difficulty accessing transport, and inability to afford basic essentials such as food and energy. Progress has been made in tackling pensioner poverty over the past 15 years and it is encouraging that absolute levels have dropped and that Wales is now closer to the UK average than previously was the case. However, significant numbers of older people are still forced to survive on very low incomes.

Projections from the Institute of Fiscal Studies suggest that levels of poverty will not change in coming years unless new measures are introduced.[30] In fact, unless improvements are achieved in the level of the state pension, in the numbers of people supported to make their own provision for retirement, in benefit take-up and in our attitudes about and support for older people in employment we could be storing up additional problems for the future.

Age Cymru believes that we need to see a coordinated strategy and approach between the devolved administrations and the UK Government to reduce pensioner poverty in Wales and across the UK, based on a long-term commitment to progressively reduce poverty year-on-year. This must be achieved alongside measures to reduce the fiscal deficit if we are to ensure that some of the most vulnerable people in society are not to pay a heavy price for a financial crisis that was not of their making.

**Graeme Francis
is Head of Policy
and Public Affairs
at Age Cymru**

Notes   1   *Older People's Wellbeing Monitor for Wales 2009,* Welsh Assembly Government
           2   *Households Below Average Income,* Department for Work and Pensions, 2010
           3   *ibid.*
           4   *Getting On: Wellbeing in later life,* Institute for Public Policy Research (IPPR), 2009
           5   *Older People's Wellbeing Monitor for Wales,* Welsh Assembly Government, 2009
           6   *Households Below Average Income,* Department for Work and Pensions. 2010
           7   *ibid.*
           8   *Gender, marital status, and ageing: linking material, health, and social resources,* Arber, S., Journal of Ageing Studies. 2004
           9   *Households Below Average Income,* Department for Work and Pensions. 2010
        10   *Pensioners, poverty and social exclusion,* Patsios, D., Poverty and social exclusion in Britain: the millennium survey. 2006
        11   BBC News, *http://www.bbc.co.uk/news/health-11243976*
        12   This Is Money, http://www.thisismoney.co.uk/pensions/article.html?in_article_id=4262 61&in_page_id=6
        13   http://www.ma.hw.ac.uk/~roger/H2_Pensions.pdf
        14   The Independent, http://www.independent.co.uk/news/uk/politics/state-pension-is-not-enough-to-live-on-minister-admits-2038076.html 29th July 2010
        15   *General Lifestyle Survey,* Department for Work and Pensions, 2008
        16   *Family Resources Survey,* Department for Work and Pensions, 2009 (from www.poverty.org.uk)
        17   The Telegraph, http://www.telegraph.co.uk/finance/personalfinance/pensions/79362 56/Linking-pensions-to-CPI-breaches-human-rights.html
        18   Written answer, Hansard, 20 July 2009, cols 852-3
        19   Tabulation Tool, Department for Work and Pensions, February 2010 http://83.244.183.180/100pc/tabtool.html
        21   *Labour Market Statistics,* ONS, July 2010
        22   *ibid.*
        23   *Living in the 21st Century: older people in England,* English Longitudinal Study of Ageing (Wave 3), Institute of Fiscal Studies, 2008
        24   ICM Research survey for One Voice report, Age UK, 2009
        25   ICM Opinion poll for Age Cymru, February 2010
        26   *Family Resources Survey United Kingdom 2007/08,* Department for Work and Pensions
        27   *Consumer and Business Attitudes to Cheques Survey 2009,* cheque and credit clearing company http://www.chequeandcredit.co.uk/resources/-/page/market_research/
        28   *Spotlight Report,* Help the Aged, 2008
        29   *Turned Away: older people and insurance,* Research Briefing, Age Concern and Help the Aged, January 2010
        30   *The IFS Green Budget,* eds Chote, R., Emmerson, C. and Shaw, J., Institute for Fiscal Studies, 2010

Stay young at heart

Margaret's story

This is the story of Margaret Williams, who runs an older people's social and education group in Trelewis. 'Stay Young at Heart' provides older members of the community with a place to relax and socialise as well as learn new skills and discuss the issues affecting them.

"One year before I was due to retire there was a sudden death in the family that changed all of our plans. My husband and I had been planning for a long time about what we were going to do when we retired but this changed everything. My husband became unwell and I took care of him.

A year later in 1986 a woman came to the house and explained she was trying to set up a club for local women in Trelewis. She was the coordinator between Trelewis and Bargoed and asked me if I would be Treasurer for the Trelewis group. Within a few months I was chairing the group as the woman didn't last very long, and I have been doing it ever since.

Within a few months I was chairing the group

Crossroads were very helpful as they came over to sit with my husband on a Monday so I was able to go to the club. My husband died ten years ago and since then I have become involved in all sorts of groups and forums in the community.

Stay Young at Heart was one of the first groups to join Voluntary Action Merthyr Tydfil (VAMT) and I have received two VAMT awards including Adult Learner of the Year. I am the chair person of a 50+ forum, I sit on the Communities First board, I am a member of Care and Repair and I am working with the local authority on the Keep Well, Keep Warm campaign. I think all this stems from being part of Stay Young at Heart.

I have met so many people through all these groups and become involved in so many different areas of the community. Although I have no family in the local area I have a lot of friends. We go on trips together, support each other and get involved in the local community.

At Stay Young at Heart we try to offer more than just bingo, which is all a lot of the clubs do. We have a speaker or practical session every week and it could be on history, gardening or card making, you name it we do it! All the members learn something. As far as I am aware we are the only club like this in Merthyr for older people, which is a shame.

we are currently campaigning against the phasing out of cheques

As well as the club I am also part of the Older People's Advice Forum where we are currently campaigning against the phasing out of cheques. If this happens in 2018 I don't know how we will pay for everything. All our payments are made by cheque at the moment and I don't want to have to keep cash around and we won't be able to pay everything by card. I have organised a petition and we have a lot of support so far.

Next year I will have been Chair of Stay Young at Heart for 25 years. Dot, our Treasurer, is the only other member who has been there since the start. Hopefully we will be doing something to celebrate."

Spoken by Margaret Williams,
and compiled by the Bevan Foundation

3.   EDUCATION

Educational equity and school performance in Wales
David Egan

This chapter considers the nature, extent and causes of the inequity which exists in educational achievement by students in the school system in Wales. It moves on to look at evidence on how gaps in student achievement can best be narrowed and then sets out specific proposals on how the Welsh Assembly Government might develop an appropriate strategy to address this major weakness of the educational system in Wales.

The achievement gap in Wales

Whilst a plethora of data exists on the achievement gap in education in Wales, it is dispersed and has not been brought together and placed in the public domain in the way that has happened in countries such as England. Nevertheless, the indicators we have show that at the ages of seven, eleven, fourteen and sixteen students who are eligible for free schools meals (FSM) in Wales perform significantly below other students and that the gap widens as they get older. Whilst the FSM measurement is by no means a perfect one, it is the most reliable indicator we have of socio-economic disadvantage in the school population.

It is particularly noticeable that this gap is apparent by the age of seven, when FSM students are already about 21 per cent behind their more privileged peers. Throughout the key stages the biggest gaps are in the subject area of English, suggesting a major problem in the literacy skills of more disadvantaged students. By the age of fifteen, whereas nearly 62 per cent of students who are not eligible for FSM achieve five or more GCSEs at higher grades, the figure for FSM students is 28 per cent: a gap of 34 per cent.

The data we have also points to the following additional characteristics of disadvantaged students:
- Their absence and exclusion rates are much higher.
- They are less inclined to 'like school a lot'.
- They are less likely to participate in post-16 and post-19 education and training and particularly to proceed into higher education.
- They are more likely to become NEET (not in education, employment or training).
- They are much more likely to suffer long-term negative effects from having low educational qualifications and skills and, therefore, to become disadvantaged adults who will repeat this cycle of deprivation for their children.

> **at the ages of seven, eleven, fourteen and sixteen students who are eligible for free schools meals (FSM) in Wales perform significantly below other students**

International comparisons

In recent years considerable attention has been paid to the slowing of improvements in educational achievement in Wales and the unfavourable comparisons that can be made between levels of attainment of students in Wales compared to those in other parts of the United Kingdom and internationally. This was particularly highlighted in 2007 by the outcomes of the Programme of International Student Assessment (PISA). For the first time in 2006 fifteen year olds in Wales sat standardised tests in English, Mathematics and Science that were also undertaken by their peers across the countries of the OECD. The outcomes placed students in Wales as the lowest performers of the UK countries and slightly below the average performance of students in OECD countries overall. In late 2010 the outcomes of the 2009 round of tests will be known. It is expected that students in Wales will not have improved their comparative performance and there is a fear that it may even have worsened.

These disappointing outcomes should, however, be set in the context of significant overall improvements in educational achievement by students in the schools of Wales over the last twenty years. What the PISA results reflect is that improvements in these outcomes have begun to falter and continue to lag behind other countries, including the other nations of the UK. They also provide clear evidence on what we know to be a significant cause of this relative low-achievement of students in Wales and that is the influence of social and economic class. Whilst for students from more privileged backgrounds there was far less difference in performance between those in Wales and their peers in other countries, there were significant gaps in performance for more disadvantaged students. What this indicates is that firstly socio-economic background has a major influence in Wales on the performance of students and secondly, that this achievement gap is much bigger in Wales than in many other countries.

The association between socio-economic disadvantage and low educational performance is an international phenomenon, but it seems to be particularly strong in Wales. Some countries, such as Finland, Canada and Korea, appear to have overcome this relationship and many others (including England) are making steady progress in doing so. In headline terms Wales can be seen as a relatively high achieving but low equity educational system.

> **Whilst for students from more privileged backgrounds there was far less difference in performance between those in Wales and their peers in other countries, there were significant gaps in performance for more disadvantaged students**

The nature of the achievement gap in Wales

Whilst the dominant factor in explaining the achievement gap in Wales is socio-economic class, the overall picture is a little more complex than this. There are in fact three facets to it at the level of individual:

- schools;
- students in the same school;
- students, on the basis of gender, ethnicity and social class.

What this indicates is that achievement gaps exist in all schools in Wales and not only those in our most disadvantaged areas. All schools have children who are in receipt of FSM and evidence indicates whether they be in small or large numbers within a school population they do less well than their more privileged peers. In fact on the basis of research undertaken in England it is likely that when students in receipt of FSM are in larger concentrations they do better than when they make up a smaller number of the school population. For those who believe that school effects can be a strong factor in educational achievement, this may appear to be counter-intuitive.

We also know that in general terms boys achieve at relatively lower levels than girls and that some – but by no means all – black and ethnic minority students perform less well. The fact that virtually all schools in Wales (apart from six single-sex comprehensive schools) are made up of both male and female students and that an increasing number have students from black and ethnic minority backgrounds, again suggests that, along with the factors associated with FSM entitlement, the performance gap is likely to be ubiquitous and of concern to all schools. Any strategy that is devised to improve equity in educational performance in Wales should, therefore, be universal and for all schools. It should also recognise that whilst gender, ethnicity and socio-economic status are all factors in explaining overall levels of educational achievement and the performance gap, the influence of class is probably three times more powerful than the other two causative factors.

The nature of inequity in educational achievement in Wales is not, however, as straightforward as the individual influences of gender, ethnicity and class might suggest. As well as individual causative effects there are also what can be called *group effects* and these are particularly potent in explaining overall student and school performance.

Given the way that the individual effects might be expected to work in concert, it could be predicted that the three boys' secondary schools in Wales, all of which are located in areas where there is significant socio-economic deprivation and in one case where there is a sizeable ethnic minority population, would be low-performing. In fact one is actually a high performing school which tends to demonstrate the potential, noted above, for schools where there are high concentrations of disadvantaged students to do better for them than when their peers are in smaller concentrations.

It could also be anticipated that there would be a group effect in schools with a high proportion of black and ethnic minority students, many of whom are boys and which generally are situated in more deprived communities. This is true to a greater extent than the potential group effect for boys' schools, but there is also here a mixed situation in relation to performance with some of our schools where there are large numbers of ethnic minority students being relatively or absolutely high performers.

In fact the most significant group size effect in Wales is to be found in schools where there are significant concentrations of students eligible for FSM. In all of these there will be large numbers of boys and in a few relatively sizeable ethnic minority populations. Whilst again there are a small number of schools in Wales that have large FSM populations that buck the trend and perform at relatively high levels, the dominant and most prevalent factor in low performance in our schools is associated with large concentrations of students (regardless of ethnicity or gender) who are in receipt of FSM and who are from disadvantaged backgrounds. Socio-economic class in Wales is a dowry leading to low educational performance and in the vast majority of cases the more of them that bring that dowry with them to their place of education, the worse they and it will do.

> **Socio-economic class in Wales is a dowry leading to low educational performance**

Of course there is also a spatial factor to this group effect. As is the case with the experience of child poverty, which affects about 30 per cent of children in Wales, the group effect in inequity of educational achievement can be found in equal measure in disadvantaged communities in:

- The major urban areas of Wales including Cardiff, Swansea, Newport and Wrexham.
- The former industrial areas of the South Wales Valleys and particularly in the Heads of the Valleys area.
- In other pockets of poverty spread across the rest of Wales.

The causes of low educational achievement

A growing and increasingly robust corpus of research-based evidence exists on the reasons why poverty and disadvantage can lead to low educational achievement. This evidence points to the following dominant factors:

- The critical influence of the level of education of parents, particularly of the mother.
- The important influence of neighbourhoods and places, particularly in relation to disengagement of older school students (14-16 year olds) and the tendency for them to become NEET.
- The attitude held by parents and particularly young people themselves to the value of education, including their attitude to higher education.
- Resources within the home environment, particularly access to a computer and the internet.

Some of the above are factors that schools can attempt to influence, but there are others where schools, or schools alone, are not able to respond. The recently developed field of research relating to student aspirations and attitudes to progression into higher education, for example, suggest that whilst schools can play an important part, individual student, peer, family and neighbourhood influences are much stronger.

School effectiveness and low achievement

These findings can be interpreted as being implicitly, if not explicitly, critical of the field of school improvement and effectiveness research and its assertions that schools, regardless of their economic and social contexts, can make the biggest difference in determining student achievement and future educational progression. Such utopian positions may indeed have been redolent of school effectiveness approaches in the early development of the field, but they are not representative of its current position, as exemplified by the School Effectiveness Framework in Wales.

It remains the case, however, within the work on school improvement and effectiveness that a powerful body of evidence exists which asserts that individual schools can make a significant difference to student outcomes despite the challenging socio-economic circumstances they face. In Wales, as in many other countries, this appears to remain an individualistic factor: high performing schools in disadvantaged areas that appear to buck the trend and to, therefore, be 'outliers' within stratifications of school performance.

In a small number of countries this type of individual school effect has been moved up to scale so that it becomes a system-wide effect, leading to all schools, regardless of their contextual circumstances, being relatively high achieving. This suggests that school effect and a system effect can be simultaneously achieved. Schools can make a huge difference and in these successful instances they make the biggest difference of all for the most disadvantaged students and communities.

What is emerging in more mature approaches to school improvement and effectiveness is a recognition of the powerful influences upon students relating to their background, their family and peer group situations and the places they live in, which are beyond the influence of the school but which have a significant impact upon students. This should not of course become a sort of 'counsel of despair': a feeling that schools exist in some kind of vortex which sucks down their best efforts to engage and motivate students to achieve. At worst this can become an attitude of hopelessness that portrays the world outside of the schools as one that pulls students in a completely different direction to that of the school. How, given these negative influences of poor parenting, negative peer-group pressure and fractured communities, can students and schools succeed?

The schools faced by such challenges that still manage to succeed and the research-based studies that report on their success, recognise two essential truths. Firstly, that schools can make a huge difference to student outcomes and that it is critical that this is the dominant belief of all who work and study in the school community. Secondly, that this requires, however, that the school works wholeheartedly with parents, the community and with other agencies so that it gains the maximum amount of support for its internal school improvement efforts.

> **individual schools can make a significant difference to student outcomes despite the challenging socio-economic circumstances they face**

How schools in Wales are narrowing the achievement gap

A small but useful body of evidence exists on how individual schools and occasionally groups of schools have succeeded in reducing the achievement gap in Wales.

Two important studies supported by the Welsh Assembly Government and the Welsh Local Government Association in 2002 (secondary) and 2006 (primary) considered how schools in disadvantaged areas in Wales had succeeded against the odds. They pointed to the following common factors:

- The existence of a positive school culture which did not accept disadvantage as a reason for low achievement and that sets high expectations.
- The role of leadership in providing a clear purpose, monitoring learning and teaching, using data and promoting effective practice.
- The need to closely involve parents and the community in the school.
- Developing an approach to the curriculum and assessment that engaged and motivated all students.

These findings have been supported by other research studies and evidence from Estyn, the schools inspectorate in Wales. They probably do not emphasise sufficiently, however, the growing evidence we have on the importance of high quality teaching that utilises our growing knowledge on the most effective types of practice to be deployed in challenging circumstances.

This evidence and that derived from other studies strongly influenced the decision of the Welsh Assembly Government in 2006 to commit a significant amount of additional funding to the RAISE programme. This was targeted at the most disadvantaged schools in Wales and has enabled them over a four year period to implement strategies chosen by the school but approved by the Welsh Assembly Government. An ongoing independent evaluation of the programme has published interim findings and is due to publish its final report. Estyn have also produced two reports on the impact of RAISE.

These evaluations and reports recognise that the full impact of RAISE is unlikely to be seen for a number of years. Whilst this can be accepted, the general picture that is emerging, however, is one whereby some RAISE strategies were well conceived, have built upon existing successful practice and have a strong likelihood of leading to improvements in student achievement, but this is by no means the overall situation. It is almost certainly the case that in the rush to get a newly available funding opportunity out to schools to support work designed to combat the effects of disadvantage, insufficient time was spent on what approaches, known through research evidence to be effective, should have been specified and more closely quality assured.

This can be seen to reflect a wider tendency in policy making and implementation in Wales since devolution to see the Assembly Government (and local authorities) as the enabler and the local agency, in this case schools, as the autonomous implementer of policy. Whilst the intentions of such policy approaches may be laudable, they are hardly strategic and they do not represent a way of taking forward evidence-informed policy so that maximum impact can be achieved for students and citizens. It is likely, therefore, that the learning to be derived from the biggest ever funded programme to tackle educational disadvantage in Wales, will be useful in parts but limited in extent. That will be a significant missed opportunity which we should learn from in taking forward policy in this area and probably more broadly.

The key elements of a strategy

What do we know, then, particularly from the growing international evidence that we have in this area, about how to overcome the association between poverty and low educational achievement, that should have been used more extensively in RAISE and which should now inform any future strategy to narrow the achievement gap in Wales?

At the level of schools, there is an increasingly robust evidence base on how schools facing challenging circumstances can succeed to a high level. This indicates that whilst they need to adopt the same approaches that all effective schools do, they should utilise these in a way that is specifically attuned to the challenging circumstances they face.

The approaches to be used should include:

- A particular emphasis on the importance of appropriate Early Years education that focuses on both pre-school experiences and the initial phase of formal schooling. Whilst these approaches should be offered to all students and their families, it appears to be particularly important that low performance that can be associated with the child's background is tracked closely once students have begun school and that appropriate interventions take place to support the child. In Wales the importance of programmes such as Flying Start and the Foundation Phase succeeding with our most disadvantaged students will, therefore, be fundamental to any future success in this area.

there is evidence that the age phase 8 to 14 is the most critical in relation to student engagement

- Given that increasingly there is evidence that the age phase 8 to 14 is perhaps the most critical in relation to student engagement and aspirations, a stronger focus on supporting disadvantaged students through this phase of education. This appears to be the age at which they are most in danger of falling away in their aspirations, participation and achievement. If the gains that are sought from the Foundation Phase in Wales are not to be wasted there needs to be a dedicated strategy in place to support students from disadvantaged backgrounds during this period of their schooling. Evidence from the USA suggests that both high quality Early Years education and continuing support through 8 to 14 education are necessary if disadvantaged students are to achieve the 'exit velocity' that will enable them to succeed as older students and young adults. It is likely that innovations in this age phase will require changes to the practice of teachers and also to the curriculum in order to make it more attractive and appropriate, with an enhanced emphasis on basic skills.

• A 14 to 16 curriculum that engages all students, enables them to achieve their potential and is supported by intervention strategies that tackle disengagement and low aspirations. There is strong evidence that this is the tipping point in relation to students participating in education and training, including higher education, post-19. If they continue to be engaged between the ages of 14 and 16 and are able to achieve a Level 2 qualification (the equivalent of five higher grades at GCSE) then they are much more likely to proceed post 16 and then post 19. The likelihood that as a result of the Learning Pathways policy in Wales that an increasing number of young people in Wales will be offered vocational courses that will enable them to achieve a Level 2 qualification is encouraging in this respect. This places an onus, however, on ensuring that there are appropriate learning progression routes available for them at post-16 including high quality apprenticeships.

• An avoidance of tracking and streaming approaches in upper primary and lower secondary education, as this appears to increase inequity without producing overall improvements in student achievement.

• Carrying out intensive interventions to support those falling behind, through an inclusive approach that utilises specialist support within schools (SEN departments and expertise) and from other professional services, through additional learning time (both in and after school), a relentless focus on basic skills, particularly literacy and through providing additional funding to disadvantaged schools to enable them to implement such strategies.

• Collaborative working between teachers, schools and school leaders faced by challenging circumstances. The experience being gained by the 'Challenge' programme in parts of England points strongly in this direction. This could be taken forward through regional learning hubs where schools were funded to work together and to share the effective practice that they were developing.

- Developing learning and teaching approaches that are specifically aligned to the needs of disadvantaged students and which, at least in the initial stages of an improvement strategy, are specified and monitored by the school leadership.

- Ensuring that the highest possible quality teachers are recruited and retained in our most challenging schools and that they receive high quality professional support and development. This may require that particular strategies are adopted in order to attract the highest quality teachers to these schools, through incentive schemes, recruitment programmes such as Teach First and the deployment of highly accomplished teachers (Advanced Skills Teachers) to lead professional development programmes at school level.

> **Ensuring that the highest possible quality teachers are recruited and retained in our most challenging schools**

- Changing the culture of a low performing school through raising expectations. This may require that high quality leaders are developed and deployed specifically to use the talents they have in succeeding in challenging circumstances. It may also necessitate accountability systems that place emphasis on the presence of such positive cultures.

Wider perspectives

These approaches are essentially ones that are school focused and located. As has been recognised above they will need to be integrated with wider approaches and interventions that focus upon families and communities as well as students if the effect of poverty on educational achievement is to be fully combated. In recent years two particular areas of policy and research have considerably added to our understanding of these factors. These are concerned firstly with the issue of student aspirations and secondly, the influence of place and neighbourhood on student and school performance.

Evidence relating to student aspirations has already been referred to above. There have been a number of significant studies in this area including one undertaken for the Cabinet Office in 2009 and a report in 2010 from the Joseph Rowntree Foundation (JRF) that draws upon longitudinal surveys of student experience.

The former study pointed to a number of critical issues, including the difficulty being faced in engaging white working-class boys in the education process and the change which appears to take place in the aspirations of working-class children in the later years of primary and early years of secondary schooling. The JRF study gives further support to the second of these findings, suggesting that student aspirations change considerably in the latter years of primary schooling and that secondary schools are left to catch up, which generally they are not able to do.

Both studies point to the importance of place and neighbourhood in influencing student attitudes, behaviour and aspirations and this is supported by evidence from other fields of research. What this suggests is that if attempts to narrow the achievement gap are to succeed they need to take significant account of the personal and cultural influences upon students in disadvantaged communities and of the importance of place itself. This suggests that there is a context-specificity to this work that necessitates that community as well as national approaches should be taken.

This has become the thinking behind the Challenge programme in England that operates in London, Greater Manchester and the Black Country. It is also behind the development in Wales of the Heads of the Valleys Education Programme which includes a Heads of the Valleys Learning Challenge. In these approaches the following components can be seen to be in place:

- An attractive learning offer to young people that attempts to motivate them and to raise their learning aspirations so that they can fulfil their potential, participate for as long as possible in education and achieve to a high level.

- Support for school effectiveness using the body of knowledge we have on how schools in these communities can succeed to a high level, which draws from a national programme but which is aligned to the situation in the area and is founded upon school-to-school collaboration.

- In order that education can play a major role in community regeneration, the integration of all policy areas and funding streams which influence education and skills (for example Communities First, the Child Poverty Strategy, 21st Century Schools, Heads of the Valleys Economic Strategy, the University of the Heads of the Valleys Institute) so that the greatest amount of support can be given to efforts to improve participation and achievement in education and thereby to narrow the gap.

The strategy

If Wales is to cease to be a 'high achievement: low equity' nation and to join the growing numbers of countries which can claim to have eradicated the association between poverty and low educational achievement, a high level strategy should be put in place by the Welsh Assembly Government. The essential elements of that strategy should be:

1. That it operates at a number of levels:
   - For all schools, because in all of them there will be instances of low student achievement that is caused by particular sets of circumstances.
   - For schools where specific gender and ethnicity issues are faced.
   - For schools where there are significant concentrations of students who are eligible for FSM and where the socio-economic disadvantage that this indicates is the major cause of low achievement.

2. That for each of these levels guidance should be provided for schools on how they can best address the needs of low-achieving students. This guidance already exists elsewhere and could easily be adapted to suit the needs of Wales. It should allow schools to build upon existing successful practice, but it should also set out evidence-informed strategies that are known to work in improving the achievement of disadvantaged students and which, therefore, would be expected to be used. There will be objections to such specification and the National Strategy-type approach that they represent. These have to be countered, based on the experience of RAISE and in the belief that it is only through such approaches that significant improvement can be achieved at a system-wide level in Wales.

3. That it should reflect the evidence that now exists on the importance of student aspirations and of area-based approaches through the development of:

   - Interventions that seek to influence the attitudes of students and their families in the latter years of primary schooling and in the 14-16 age group (to encourage post-16 participation).

   - Other area-based challenge approaches to accompany the Heads of the Valleys Learning Challenge.

Implementing the strategy

It could be said to be a reasonable criticism of education policy – and perhaps other policy areas – since devolution that we have become policy rich and implementation poor. If a strategy that is intended to improve equity in educational outcomes in our schools is to succeed then it is equally important that we develop innovative and effective approaches to implementing the strategy.

To this end it can be suggested that the strategy should have three phases:
- A *Development Phase* (immediate).
- An *Implementation Phase* (2011-2016)
- An *Evaluation Phase* (ongoing with reporting milestones).

The development phase should see the following being put in place:

- A *Narrowing the Achievement Gap* team should be established by the Welsh Assembly Government. This team should be made up of experienced educational professionals who have an established track record in this area and of policy experts in this field. They should be charged to develop at high speed a Narrowing the Achievement Gap Strategy that is innovative, well founded on evidence and which can be implemented from September 2011.

- The team should commission a rapid evidence assessment exercise to bring together all the available, but currently dispersed, evidence on the attainment gap in Wales. The DCSF publication 'Deprivation and Education: The Evidence on Pupils in England, Foundation Stage to Key Stage 4' should be seen as a template for this work.

- A Reference Group should be created to bring together policy leads in the Welsh Assembly Government's Department for Children, Education and Lifelong Learning, stakeholder groups and other interested parties. The purpose of this group would be as a testing ground for policy development work undertaken by the team, but not to undertake such work itself.

- The team and the Reference Group should ensure that the strategy developed is aligned to the School Effectiveness Framework, the Child Poverty Strategy for Wales, the outcomes of the final evaluation of RAISE, Estyn inspection evidence, the corpus of educational research in this area and the statistical evidence commissioned through the rapid evidence assessment.

- Notwithstanding the above, the team and the Reference Group would be remitted to produce a strategy that incorporated the three approaches set out above in the section 'the Strategy'.

- Within the area-based approach that a *learning offer* should be constructed around the following:
  - The provision of high quality pre-school child and family support.
  - A curriculum that engages and motivates students.
  - Support for the wellbeing of young people in order to foster their aspirations and self-esteem.
  - The promotion of personal, social and commercial approaches to enterprise, entrepreneurism and employability.
  - A strong focus on basic skills including functional literacy.
  - Enhanced opportunities for the most able and talented.
  - Out-of-hours learning.
  - Developing the quality of teaching and leadership.

The **implementation phase** should lead to the following:

- In April 2011 the team should publish a high level policy document setting out the strategy and how it will be implemented.

- Thereafter a rigorous project development plan should be developed to facilitate implementation from September 2011.

- The materials that will be needed to assist all schools in Wales in closing the achievement gap should be adapted from those currently available elsewhere.

- The area-based approach should be initially developed in a single area of Wales, chosen to complement the work already underway in the Heads of the Valleys Challenge and thereby possibly located in South West or North Wales. This should be a community based and located initiative that utilises an innovative policy delivery mechanism.

The **policy evaluation phase** should begin from the summer term of 2010 and continue throughout the life of the strategy, reporting at key points such that it is able to influence its ongoing development. The nature of the evaluation should be highly innovative and represent a commitment by the Welsh Assembly Government to make a step-change in the utilisation of evidence-informed policy.

Conclusion

The current strong, enduring and symbiotic association between poverty and low educational achievement in Wales represents nothing less than a blight on our nation, the life-chances of a significant number of its citizens and the wider aspirations of the Welsh Assembly Government to create a prosperous country at ease with itself.

We should have the confidence to believe that we can overcome this insidious and enervating aspect of our national identity. As the Canadian educationalist Ben Levin points out, in learning as in other areas of achievement, we do not yet know what the boundaries of student capability are.

In order to release the immense untapped potential of the young people of Wales and for education to make the contribution it can to a just and equitable society, we should consider the type of strategy argued for above and a modus operandi that can bring it to life in a way that would transform educational achievement in Wales.

We know how to do it. What we need now is the resolution to use that knowledge.

> **The current strong, enduring and symbiotic association between poverty and low educational achievement in Wales represents nothing less than a blight on our nation**

References   Ainscow, M. and West, M. (2006) 'Drawing out the lessons: leadership and collaboration' in Ainscow, M and West, M. *Improving Urban Schools*. Open University Press: Maidenhead

Ainscow, M. (2009) 'Local solutions for local contexts: the development of more inclusive education systems' in Alenkaer, R. *Leadership Perspectives in the Inclusive School*. Frydenlund: Copenhagen

Barber, M. and Mourshed, M. (2007) *How The World's Best-Performing Schools Systems Come Out On Top*. London: McKinsey and Company

Bradshaw, J., Sturman, L., Vappula, H., Ager, R. and Wheater, R. (2007) *Achievement of 15 Year Olds in Wales:PISA 2006 National Report*. Slough: National Foundation for Educational Research

Brook, A. (2008) *Raising Education Achievement and Breaking the Cycle of Inequality in the United Kingdom*. OECD:Paris

Cabinet Office (2008) *Aspiration and Attainment Amongst Young People in Deprived Communities*. Cabinet Office: London

Cassen, R. and Kingdon, G. (2007) *Tackling Low Educational Achievement*. Joseph Rowntree Foundation: York

Centre for Research on the Wider Benefits of Learning (2008) *The Social and Personal Benefits of Learning*. Institute of Education: London

Davidson, J. (2006) 'Pathways Out of Poverty', *Agenda*: Journal of the Institute of Welsh Affairs, Summer 2006.

Department of Children, Schools and Families (2008) *The Extra Mile: How Schools Succeed in Raising Aspirations in Deprived Communities*. DCSF: London

Egan, D. (2006). 'Educating for Social Justice', *Agenda*: Journal of the Institute of Welsh Affairs, Spring 2006.

Egan, D. (2007) *Combating Child Poverty in Wales: Are Appropriate Education Policies in Place?* York: Joseph Rowntree Foundation.

Egan, D. and Marshall, S. (2007) 'Educational Leadership and School Renewal in Wales', *Australian Journal of Education*, 51:3, November 2007.

Egan, D. (2008) *Why Not the Best Schools? The Wales Report* ACER Press: Victoria

Estyn (2008) *The Impact of RAISE*. Cardiff:Estyn

Estyn (2009) *Local Authorities and Schools Causing Concern*. Cardiff:Estyn

Estyn (2009) *The Impact of RAISE 2008-09* Cardiff: Estyn

Estyn (2010) Tackling Child Poverty and Disadvantage in Schools. Estyn: Cardiff

Goodman, A. and Gregg, P. (2010) *Poorer Children's Educational Attainment: How Important Are Attitudes and Behaviour?* Joseph Rowntree Foundation: York

Hirsch, D. (2007) *Experiences of Poverty and Educational Disadvantage*. Joseph Rowntree Foundation: York

Holtom, D. (2008) Evaluation of RAISE: Interim Report. Abergavenny: People and Work Unit

Holtom, D. (2008) Evaluation of RAISE: Thematic Report on the Work of Regional Coordinators. Abergavenny: People and Work Unit

Holtom, D. (2009) External Evaluation of RAISE; Thematic Report on Options for Sustaining the Impact of RAISE. Abergavenny: People and Work Unit

Holtom, D. (2009) Evaluation of RAISE: 2nd Interim Report. Abergavenny: People and Work Unit

James, C., Connolly, M., Dunning, G. & Elliot, T. (2006). *How Very Effective Primary Schools Work*. London: Paul Chapman Publishing

Kenway, P., Parsons, N., Carr, J., and Palmer, G. (2005) *Monitoring Poverty and Social Exclusion in Wales 2005*. London: Joseph Rowntree Foundation/New Policy Institute.

Kenway, P. and Palmer, G. (2007) *Monitoring Poverty and Social Exclusion in Wales 2007*. York: Joseph Rowntree Foundation.

Levin, B. (2007) 'Enduring Issue in Urban Education': *Journal of Comparative Policy Analysis.*

Levin, B. (2008) *How To Change 5000 Schools*. Harvard Education Press: Cambridge, Ma.

Ofsted (2009) *Twelve Outstanding Secondary School Excelling Against the Odds*. Ofsted: London

Reynolds, D., Stringfield, S. and Schaffer, E. (2006) 'The High Reliability School Project: Some Preliminary Results and Analyses' in Chrispeels, J. and Harris, A. (Eds) *School Improvement: International Perspectives*. London: Routledge.

Stringfield, S., Reynolds, D. and Schaffer, E. (2008) *Improving Secondary Students' Academic Achievement Through A Focus on Reform Reliability*. CFBT.

Sutton Trust (2008) *Increasing Higher Education Participation Amongst Disadvantaged*

Young People and Schools in Poor Communities. Sutton Trust: London

Sutton Trust (2008) *Wasted Talent? Attrition Rates of High Achieving Pupils Between School and University*. Sutton Trust: London

Sutton Trust (2009) *Attainment Gaps Between Pupils in the Most Deprived and Advantaged Schools*. Sutton Trust: London

Tough, P. (2009) *Whatever It Takes*. New York: First Mariner Books

The Education Trust (2009) *What States Can Do to Improve Teacher Effectiveness. Washington: The Education Trust*

Welsh Assembly Government. (2002) *Narrowing the gap in the performance of schools.* Cardiff: Welsh Assembly Government

Welsh Assembly Government. (2005) *Narrowing the gap in the performance of schools project: Phase 2 primary schools.* Cardiff: Welsh Assembly Government.

Welsh Assembly Government (2008) *School Effectiveness Framework: Building Effective Learning Communities Together.* Cardiff: Welsh Assembly Government

Welsh Assembly Government (2008) *The Child Wellbeing Monitor for Wales*. Welsh Assembly Government: Cardiff

Welsh Assembly Government (2009) *Academic Achievement and Entitlement to Free School Meals 2008*. Welsh Assembly Government: Cardiff

Welsh Assembly Government (2009) *Task and Finish Group on 8-14 Education Provision in Wales: First Stage Report*. Cardiff: Welsh Assembly Government

Welsh Assembly Government (2010) *Child Poverty Strategy for Wales.* Cardiff: Welsh Assembly Government

Whelan, F. (2009) *Lessons Learned: How Good Policies Produce Better Schools.* London: Author.

Wilkinson, R. and Pickett, K. (2009) *The Spirit Level: Why More Equal Societies Almost Always Do Better.* London: Allen Lane

Making my life **worth living again**

Mark's story

NIACE (the National Institute of Adult Continuing Education) is the national, independent organisation for adult learning in England and Wales. NIACE both represents and advances the interests of all adult learners and potential learners – especially those who have benefited least from education and training. NIACE aims to improve opportunities for adult learners across all sectors with a particular focus on those adults who have not had successful access to learning in their initial education. NIACE Dysgu Cymru, the Welsh arm of NIACE, conducts work in Wales. NIACE Dysgu Cymru hosts the annual Inspire! Adult Learner of the Year awards, celebrating the incredible achievements of learners, and highlighting the power of learning as a tool for overcoming the most challenging obstacles.

Mark Atkinson won the Higher Education Learner of 2009 award, and explains how learning helped him overcome years of poverty, alcohol and drug abuse.

"Just five short years ago, I was living in an extremely poorly erected tent (twenty quid from Argos!), with no sleeping-bag, in the sand dunes of Harlech, a small seaside town in North Wales. The course of events which led me to this low point included over twenty years of addiction to alcohol, Class 'A' drugs and, quite bizarrely, literature. Strangely, throughout the five months, between January and May (Brrrrrr!) that I spent attempting to stop the tent from succumbing to the effects of gale-force winds and sandstorms, my sanity was sustained (allegedly), by poetry. Having no pen or paper to hand, I began to compose poems, 'Tennyson-style', in my head. It had long been my ambition to study English at university, with a view to one day becoming a published author. Things,

> I was living in an extremely poorly erected tent with no sleeping-bag

however, weren't looking promising for the realization of this at that juncture!

Fate smiled on me for the umpteenth time, in the shape of The Elim Church in Barmouth. The church's Pastor, the Reverend Dawn Robinson, had heard of my plight and secured me a flat, where I lived for a year, and eventually, a place in a rehabilitation centre in Aberystwyth. During my six month stay at the centre, I was given the opportunity to rebuild my life, and also to put 'finger to keyboard' and get my poetic musings down in pixel-form.

An interesting meeting with Clive Donovan, the representative of the out-reach program, TRAC, resulted in an interview with Doctors Sue Pester and Debra Croft of the Mid and West Wales Widening Access Partnership. Both Sue and Debra seemed to recognize some long-hidden potential in me (despite hearing some of my poetry!), and recommended that I enrol for the Aberystwyth Summer University, with a view to beginning a degree course the following year. This I did, and it proved to be a great success, infusing me with the self-confidence that I'd lost through years of substance misuse.

I continued to write poetry, during my time at the Summer University, and then, after being accepted to study for a degree in English and Creative Writing at Aberystwyth University, I was nominated for, and received the NIACE Dysgu Cymru Adult Learner of the Year Award for the whole of Wales...cool!

my poems were recently short-listed in a national poetry competition

With my ego now gigantic, and my confidence suitably bolstered by the NIACE Dysgu Cymru Award and my successful first year at university, I began attending an evening poetry class and participating in public poetry readings, both organized by Julie Yonkman of Aberystwyth's School of Lifelong Learning. These readings convinced me of my literary 'worth,' giving me the incentive to not only submit my work to various competitions and publications, but also to organize my own evening of poetry, entitled 'PLANET POETIKA!' on the 6th of October this 2010. The event was made possible through Aberystwyth University's Open Platform Scheme, which allows up-and-coming performers and artistes access to facilities in order to give them the start that they wouldn't otherwise have had. I've picked five wickedly talented local poets, all hungry for success, to join me and to showcase their talents, on what promises to be a dynamic, diverse and entertaining evening. I even managed to persuade my friend, Marvel Comics writer and artist, Nick Abadzis, to supply the artwork that I'm using in all the publicity…a truly nice bloke (he said, shamelessly name-dropping!).

As the happy end, to what promised at the start, to be a depressing and depressingly sordid tale of sadness and woe (yes 'woe!'), my poems were recently short-listed in a national poetry competition, and one in particular, entitled 'Me Dad' is to be published in an annual poetry anthology, 'The Book of Dreams,' (available at all good bookshops….blah blah blah!).

I'd really like to thank NIACE Dysgu Cymru and the very special people I've mentioned above. You've all had a massive part in making my life worth living once again…cheers! I'd especially like to thank my partner, Lottie, whom I plan to marry in July next year (or as soon as I can afford a ring…whichever comes first!). You've quite literally *saved* my life!

For more information about NIACE Dysgu Cymru's campaigns visit: www.niacedc.org.uk/campaigns.

For more information about Mark's story see: http://www.youtube.com/user/niacedc#p/u/37/922d9qNXBmM

The Loners' Club

By Mark Atkinson

Every night I hold a meeting
where the members number one.
I share my thoughts and feelings
till my cup of coffee's gone.
I've considered advertising,
once put a poster in the pub,
but no-one seemed inclined to join
the Loners' Club

It's hard to hold a meeting when
you're the only person there.
When everybody hates your guts,
condemns and judges when you share.
I thought of tele-conferencing
but I was scared I'd get a snub.
It's so hard being founder-member
of the Loners' Club.

Some people call me misfit,
some people say I'm strange.
I'd like to see *them* do *my* job,
with all I've to arrange.
There's literature and pamphlets,
I even collect the subs.
Yes, it's a full time occupation
In the Loners' Club.

So if you'd like to join us loners,
the membership is free.
All you need's an empty life,
you too can live like me!
We can go on separate outings,
watch our flats become the hub
of thriving isolation.
That's the Loners' Club.

4.

HOUSING

Raising the roof?
Housing, poverty
and social exclusion

Tamsin Stirling

'HOME IS WHERE THE HEART IS' goes the saying. But for many people in Wales, home is distinctly unwelcoming; for others, it does not exist in any meaningful sense and, for some, home does not exist at all. The links between housing, poverty and social exclusion are clear. Though the number of individuals involved is small, rough sleeping is probably the most extreme form of social exclusion. Living in poor quality housing impacts significantly on quality of life, e.g. by contributing to poor physical and mental health, increasing income spent on keeping warm etc. Households on low incomes have far fewer housing options than wealthier households, are unlikely to be able to fulfil the property-owning expectation of the majority and are more likely to be reliant on state support for payment of rent, which in itself creates a further poverty trap. And we know that, through no fault of their own, the most vulnerable people can end up in the worst quality housing in the private rented sector with the poorest standards of management.

> **Living in poor quality housing impacts significantly on quality of life**

In recent years, the links between housing, poverty and social exclusion have become ever more entangled. What have come to be seen as highly irresponsible lending practices were at the centre of the credit crunch as bundled-up sub-prime mortgages spread their 'toxicity' across the financial world. Lending to people who could not afford to pay their mortgages turned out to be a really bad idea, not just for those individuals, but for the finance industry and the economy more broadly. And the results of these practices are being played out in recession, cuts in public investment and job losses – which will loop back to more households struggling to exist on low incomes. We've seen the expectation of continuously rising house values shaken to its core and the main model for securing affordable housing through the planning system (section 106 agreements) undermined.

A bit of reflection

Wales has some distinctive characteristics in terms of housing – lower average house prices and a higher level of owner-occupation than most other parts of the UK, with many home-owners living on low incomes. In physical terms, our terraced housing is also distinctive, but in some areas, is over-prevalent, forming what could be termed a housing 'mono-culture'.

Thinking back to the mid 1980s, we have much to celebrate. The winners of the various Welsh housing awards each year are testament to the energy and innovation across the housing sector in Wales. There are great examples of involving tenants and communities in their housing and environment, the building of new sustainable homes, work to enable affordable housing in rural communities, the regeneration of estates, preventing and tackling homelessness, collaboration between organisations – the list is long.

In the past twenty years, the housing sector has built many new homes for people who cannot afford to buy their own place in the open housing market. The quality of many homes in both the social and private sectors has been improved, with the Welsh Housing Quality Standard providing the framework for the social sector and housing renewal areas acting as a driver for the private sector, albeit with action being concentrated in small areas.

In recent years, housing investment has been linked to the creation of local jobs and support for local economies – the housing-led regeneration agenda. Wales also has a vigorous supported housing sector, providing accommodation, support and learning opportunities to people with a wide range of needs in ways that simply did not happen 20 years ago.

The shape of the social housing sector has changed out of all recognition through stock transfer, with tenants in 11 local authority areas voting to transfer their homes to a new registered social landlord since 2003. Four out of the eleven transfer organisations are community mutuals, a form of organisation with community ownership and a high degree of accountability to members. All of the transfer organisations see themselves explicitly as housing and regeneration agencies, with remits far broader than the traditional landlord role.

The private rented sector is now recognised as an essential part of the housing market, facilitating labour mobility and providing housing choice. It is also a sector which is increasingly being called on to house people on lower incomes and with support needs, as well as those who, on the face of

The UK's first zero-carbon Passive House developed in 2010 by United Welsh in Ebbw Vale

it, are able to afford home ownership, but are currently unable to access mortgage finance. Overall, the size of the private rented sector has increased, with forecasts that it could become larger than the council and housing association sectors added together within a few years. Initiatives to improve the quality of the private rented sector such as a Wales-wide landlord accreditation scheme[1] are to be welcomed.

major challenges face many young people trying to find somewhere decent to live

The environmental impact of housing has started to be addressed, with ambitious sustainability standards set for new housing. The challenge of retro-fitting the existing housing stock is significant and progress is slower here, although pilots have been undertaken on traditional terraced housing, including a scheme in Penrhiwceiber.

But we also have much pondering to do. Homelessness is still very much with us, there are still people living in unsuitable and unacceptable housing conditions across Wales, major challenges face many young people trying to find somewhere decent to live and many people cannot sustain or maintain their homes.

In terms of whether we have enough housing to meet need in Wales, in 2010, research commissioned by the Welsh Assembly Government and undertaken by Cambridge University, found that an estimated 284,000 additional homes are required in Wales between 2006 and 2026, 183,000 of these in the market sector and 101,000 in the non-market sector[2]. These estimates average 14,200 dwellings a year – 9,200 in the market sector and 5,100 in the non-market sector (this non-market figure compares to 2,500 a year when Alan Holmans looked at the situation in 2003). The current backlog of unmet housing need is estimated at 9,500 households. These figures make the 6,500 additional affordable homes target over the lifetime of the current Assembly administration set out in *One Wales* look somewhat less than ambitious.

We still spend significant amounts of money on emergency accommodation for people who have nowhere to go and, despite efforts to reduce the use of B&B accommodation, its use remains, particularly for those whose behaviour is seen as challenging. At the time of writing, the author has recently attended a series of workshops around Wales looking at how services for homeless and potentially homeless 16 and 17 year olds can be improved. At each event, local authorities have said that they use B&B for homeless young people with challenging behaviour due to a lack of other appropriate options.

Many areas in Wales have seen significant falls in house prices. On the face of it, this might have been expected to make things easier for first time buyers. However, the majority of mortgage products that used to be readily available are now judged 'too risky' and have been withdrawn. 100 per cent mortgages are no longer available and interest rates for borrowing are very much slanted in favour of those who are able to put up a large deposit. Most councils and housing associations are reporting large increases in the numbers of households registering on their waiting lists for rented accommodation, with a total of over 97,000 people across Wales on waiting lists while, at the same time, fewer of these rented properties are becoming empty each year as more tenants are staying put.

The proportion of Welsh households owning their home has stayed relatively static at around 72 per cent. However, through initiatives to encourage lower income households to buy their home, most significantly the Right to Buy and the lending practices referred to earlier, there are more home-owners who could be described as 'asset rich, but cash poor' than there were 25 years ago. And for those who bought before the last slump in prices, their ability to sell their way out of trouble will be extremely limited. Analysis published by Roof magazine noted that Welsh house prices fell by an average of nearly 13 per cent between 2007 and 2009 but that the average deposit required to buy had risen from just over £11,000 in 2007 to over £24,000 in 2009. So whilst in income terms, households may be able to afford to buy, without a substantial deposit they simply won't be able to get access to a mortgage. No wonder the average age of first-time buyers is now 35.

> **Our 20th and 21st century love affair with owner-occupation appears to have created a particular vulnerability to the impact of the credit crunch**

The interconnectedness of the housing market and the economy has become all too evident. Our 20th and 21st century love affair with owner-occupation, creating what Professor Martin Daunton termed the 'property-owning democracy', appears to have created a particular vulnerability within the UK to the impact of the credit crunch. And the context in Wales is a higher level of owner-occupation than other parts of the UK, with many of these owner-occupiers being on low incomes.

An eye to the future

So what might the future hold for Welsh housing and those on low incomes? On the face of it, the outlook is grim. Until now, the Welsh Assembly Government has always had a rising budget; this financial year, the trend has ceased and will go rapidly into reverse from next financial year onwards. Housing should not expect to escape reductions in either capital or revenue budgets. More broadly, with greater reliance on the public sector and a higher proportion of the working population having jobs in the public sector, Wales is particularly vulnerable to cuts in public sector investment. And the public and private sectors are not hermetically sealed off from each other; we have already seen the demise of one major private sector housing contractor, Connaught, whose main business in Wales was providing services to local authorities and housing associations. There is also the delicate issue of the end of European Structural Funds in 2013. Although by definition, not much of this goes directly into housing, the impact will be felt as many housing-related community development projects across Wales have benefitted from financial support from the Structural Funds.

Given the devolution settlement, Wales will feel the effects of part of the

Westminster coalition government agenda, despite different policy directions here. A key example is the package of changes to the housing benefit system proposed in advance of the October 2010 Comprehensive Spending Review. Analysis by the Welsh Local Government Association has concluded that the changes will affect the majority of Housing Benefit claimants in Wales, reducing the support that they receive through the housing benefit system[3]. Some households will be affected by a number of the changes. The October 2010 Comprehensive Spending Review determined the overall funding settlement for Wales, as well as policy direction on non-devolved matters such as welfare benefits. For housing organisations, it will be important to consider how proposals and funding announcements interconnect, in order to work out how best to respond in terms of business priorities and how to work with communities.

> **We may see increasing housing demand from young people, including homelessness, at a time when there is less public money available to build new social housing**

Widespread concern has been expressed about the implications of changes in welfare and housing benefits in terms of increased homelessness, more young people being asked to leave the family home etc. We may see increasing housing demand from young people, including homelessness, at a time when there is less public money available to build new social housing or provide relevant support services. And if a young person rents their own home and is not able to get a job within 12 months, they will face a reduction in their Housing Benefit which they will need to make up from their already very low income.

The Westminster Government is highly committed to reforming both housing benefit and the wider welfare benefit system, with the emphasis on getting people off benefit and into work. The underlying context for the changes is the desire to significantly reduce the Housing Benefit bill which currently runs at an annual cost of around £20 billion.

We now know that capital investment for affordable housing in England has been cut by around 50 per cent, with new 'flexible tenancies' at intermediate rents of 80 per cent of market rents being proposed in order to maintain supply. However, there is a clear tension between increased rents and the desire to significantly reduce the Housing Benefit bill. Given that housing is devolved, the Welsh Assembly Government does not need to follow English policies on social housing tenancies or rent levels. However, further changes to the welfare benefit system contained in the spending review will impact on many people in Wales. A clear example is the increase in the age threshold for the Shared Room Rate in Housing Benefit from 25 to 35 years of age. The rationale for this change is that 'young' people living in the private rented sector should not be advantaged over other tenures. In the words of the spending review document itself, this *'will ensure that Housing Benefit rules reflect the housing expectations of people of a similar age not on benefits'* So the outcomes of what is acknowledged as a highly dysfunctional home ownership market are informing the detail of policy for other tenures. Somewhat twisted logic.

So, it is clear that, over the coming years, money is going to be extremely tight for individuals across Wales and for housing organisations trying to meet housing need. Might necessity be the motherhood of invention?

Some thinking is underway about how capital investment in affordable housing might be undertaken in a different way from the current mechanism of Social Housing Grant through the establishment of a Welsh Housing Investment Trust, involving a bond style of investment[4]. The technicalities of developing this model are intriguing and the development may bring new sources of investment into housing. However, I am concerned that a holistic view is not being taken. In the understandable rush to ensure more output for less public investment, the result could be increased rents which would mean a greater poverty trap for those on low incomes, particularly in the light of the proposed changes to housing and welfare benefits.

Housing organisations with land, particularly the stock transfer organisations, may be able to develop new affordable housing without the need for Social Housing Grant, (or other input of capital from government), and new building techniques which produce homes with lower CO_2 emissions can be highly cost effective. New types of partnership between housing organisations with land and developers may also prove effective in adding to the number of affordable homes across Wales, but will require different ways of working. For example, a housing organisation transfers land to a developer under an agreement that when properties are built, a proportion will be in the ownership of the housing organisation to rent as affordable housing.

And of course there are the 26,000 plus homes across Wales that have been empty for more than 6 months, many of which could be brought back into use. Some good work is already underway on this, with practical partnerships between local authorities, housing associations and the owners of the properties[5]. However, the often-used model of grants to home-owners will need to be replaced by approaches through which money is recycled such as loans, in line with the emphasis in the Welsh Assembly Government's economic development strategy, *Economic Renewal: a new direction*, which was published in July 2010.[6]

Another resource which could be brought into the mix is publicly-owned land. If the need for more affordable housing is identified as a priority both nationally and locally, publicly-owned land could be released at below market (or even nil) cost. This is simply a different take on current debates around asset transfer, particularly if the land were transferred to Community Land Trusts, organisations established at community level to acquire land and other fixed assets and hold these in perpetuity for the benefit of the local community.

And while the need for additional affordable housing requires focus, we should not forget low income home-owners. High levels of low income

> **there are the 26,000 plus homes across Wales that have been empty for more than 6 months**

home ownership combined with increased longevity is a new social phenomenon, one which requires national policy recognition as well as innovation in the provision of information, advice and support and financial products that work for these households. The Housing Action Charity (HACT) has recognised this and has established a project called Fit for Living to look at this issue[7]. One of the elements of the project is examining what role registered social landlords/housing associations might take in relation to supporting older low income home-owners, e.g. providing repairs services to such households, offering them the opportunity to purchase components such as windows, doors and boilers at cost etc.

An ageing population is not the only challenging demographic for Welsh housing. Statistics Wales has calculated that households led by lone parents will increase from 102,000 in 2008 to more than 172,000 if present trends continue[8]. This is likely to intensify housing pressure.

We will need to do some new thinking about models of accommodation. We know that isolation is an increasing problem for many people of all ages, yet we concentrate on providing 'units' of accommodation for single households of various sizes. Maybe both the demographics and the degree of housing need might prompt consideration of models such as co-housing[9] and home-sharing[10], as well as more self-help options[11]. In Wales, a few examples of interesting models for people at certain stages of their lives are emerging. For example, in Newport, the council, a housing association and support provider are working together to develop a shared accommodation model for young people who are in work, providing them with a supported living environment for 18-24 months, during which time they save in order to move on to the next stage in their housing career. And perhaps attitudes towards renting will change for the positive and we will manage to make tenure-neutral housing a reality, removing the sharp and divisive distinction between owners and renters.

> **We will need to do some new thinking about models of accommodation**

Some new thinking is also needed in relation to reducing CO_2 emissions across all tenures. As noted earlier, exciting work is going on in relation to building new housing that has less impact on the environment, with additional Welsh Assembly Government funding enabling homes to be built to level 3, 4, 5 or even 6 of the Code for Sustainable Homes, level 6 being carbon neutral[12]. But there would be much to be gained from an area-based approach to insulating the existing housing stock. Such an approach could be linked to renewal areas or Communities First areas and would be an opportunity to create semi-skilled job opportunities as well as use insulation materials produced in Wales. It would be more straightforward than relying on individual households having to identify whether they are eligible for the bewildering array of grants and loans and could be combined with basic advice on energy use.

The future is going to be difficult, and particularly difficult for those on low incomes. Housing organisations will need to identify what action they can take to work with communities in order to mitigate against the impact of cuts in services. This context is also being presented as an opportunity to consider new models of service provision such as mutuals or social enterprises. However, it will be important not to set new ventures up to fail in what will be a very harsh economic environment. Mutual or co-operative structures are no guarantee in themselves of financial success.

The devolution conundrum

One of the challenges for Welsh housing is the devolution settlement. Housing is an area which has been devolved to the Welsh Assembly Government since its establishment in 1999. Sounds simple doesn't it? But the reality is rather less clear cut. Housing policy is certainly devolved and there are an increasing number of examples of policy divergence between England and Wales. On legislation, the Legislative Competency Order on housing will enable the Welsh Assembly Government to pass Measures on housing, with the first of these to be on the Right to Buy and another to follow on the regulation of social landlords. But when it comes to housing finance, things get more complex. English decisions taken in the English context currently create a financial baseline for Wales, despite a potential policy agenda mismatch. A positive referendum result on further powers for the Assembly, plus a review of the finance settlement for Wales along the lines of the recommendations of the Holtham Commission[13] will improve things significantly, but the tricky interface between the welfare benefits system and housing costs will remain.

To me, fundamentally addressing our housing conundrums seems to fall into the 'too difficult' box. Housing does not get the same political attention as health and education, at least in part because many people are adequately housed and are able to take care of their own housing needs (and those of family members). But for those who cannot access market housing, there is insufficient good quality housing which is affordable.

Competing interests around 'efficiency gains' and getting 'more from less' may mean further reductions in genuinely affordable housing. As we know from the history of housing policy, an increase in the proportion of private finance going in to new 'social' housing means higher rents to be paid by those on low incomes. In the 1980s and 1990s, 'housing benefit will take the strain' was an oft-heard response to concerns about rising rents. We cannot expect the same in the coming years.

A couple of years ago, I wondered whether we might see a positive outcome from the credit crunch shock to the economy and the housing market with a refocusing on 'housing as home' rather than 'housing as investment'. I don't think that the signs so far are particularly good.

Will the population of Wales be more or less adequately housed in 2020 than we are now? A difficult call to make. As a relatively affluent country in

> Will the population of Wales be more or less adequately housed in 2020 than we are now? A difficult call to make

the 21st century, albeit one with significant financial challenges, we certainly need a clear plan to adequately house our population. But, in the period of fiscal famine ahead, housing is likely to find itself in a difficult battle for resources. Collectively, we need to ensure that low income households across Wales are not the unwitting victims of this battle.

Tamsin Stirling
is an independent
housing consultant
and editor of Welsh
Housing Quarterly
www.whq.org.uk

Notes

1   www.welshlandlords.org.uk
2   http://new.wales.gov.uk/topics/housingandcommunity/research/housing/needandemand/?lang=en
3   www.wlga.gov.uk/english/housing-benefit
4   www.chcymru.org.uk
5   www.cih.org/cymru/policy/key9.htm
6   http://wales.gov.uk/docs/det/report/100705anewdirectionen.pdf
7   www.hact.org.uk
8   http://www.walesonline.co.uk/news/wales-news/2010/09/30/single-parent-homes-expected-to-soar-in-next-two-decades-91466-27369307/
9   http://www.cohousing.org.uk
10 http://homeshare.org/help.aspx
11 http://self-help-housing.org
12 http://new.wales.gov.uk/topics/sustainabledevelopment/design/code/?lang=en
13 http://wales.gov.uk/icffw/home/?lang=en

'Homelessness can truly happen to anyone'

James's story

James is 44. The breakdown of his marriage and redundancy after 4 years of working for a company meant that James quickly went from having a family and a job to sleeping on the sofa at his brother's house. When this became impossible, James was without help and alone on the streets.

"I was turned away from a couple of hostels in the area as I didn't have a drug or alcohol problem and people who did were prioritised. Eventually I was referred to The Wallich and stayed in their cold weather room, which is opened up during the winter as an emergency bed. Initially I said I had an alcohol problem to guarantee the room would be mine for the night but the next morning admitted this was a lie. It wasn't a problem at Julian Hodge [Centre] who accepted me purely on the basis that I had nowhere else to go. Luckily a room became available the same day and I took it.

... an incredible amount of emotional support...

I was caught in a difficult situation – fighting for access to my children whilst I was unemployed meant that I was entitled to Legal Aid, but if I started working, this benefit would stop and the wages I would be likely to earn wouldn't cover the legal fees. The Wallich, as well as a place to stay, offered me an incredible amount of emotional support for the next year. As I have a literacy problem it was hard for me to cope with letters to and from solicitors and the courts, so the workers here took care of those kind of things as well as helping me apply for permanent housing.

My stay at Julian Hodge [Centre] has been a real eye opener. There are so many reasons why people can end up on the street and so many issues that make it difficult for people to have a home of their own. Homelessness can truly happen to anyone but terms like 'dosser' are too quickly used if you say you live in a hostel. Luckily the support here has been second to none.'

James is now living in a flat of his own and has been reunited with his children.

James is a pseudonym.
Compiled by The Wallich.

5.

HEALTH

Thinking upstream
the challenge
of health inequalities in Wales
Michael Shepherd

INEQUALITIES IN HEALTH IN WALES as in the UK are widening, despite a continued rise in life expectancy. Between 1999 and 2007, for every 100 people in the UK who died aged under 65 in the richest areas, there were 212 in the poorest. The British Medical Journal (Thomas et al 2010) reported earlier this year that inequalities are now worse than in the great depression of the 1930s when, at its peak, the ratio was 100 to 191. In commenting on the report, Professor Michael Marmot, who has recently led inquiries into inequalities in health for both the World Health Organisation and the UK government, was quoted by the BBC saying:

> "There are two major challenges: to improve health for everybody and to reduce inequalities. In Britain, we have done well on the first – not on the second"
>
> (BBC News 2010).

In concluding, Thomas et al (2010) argue that inequalities in mortality rates are influenced by complex and long-term processes. They reflect the outcome of socially patterned exposures in early life and the cumulative effect of experiences in adult life.

Discussion of inequalities must take place within a social, economic and political context, which notes the traditions and the histories of countries and regions. Writing about the decline of industrial South Wales, Bennett and colleagues (2000) conclude that it represented not only a decline in the local economy, but a cultural crisis. The closure of pits and steelworks undermined a range of social networks and activities that were grounded in the workplace and in the trades unions, but also had wider importance in the life of the local community. There was, and remains, a deep sense of loss in mining and steelmaking communities which had relied on these industries for their existence for many decades. Similar conclusions are reached by Elliot et al (2010) in studying the likely impact of the current recession on communities in South Wales.

How we understand health, itself, and the construction of health is an important consideration. Our health services, it has often been said, are an illness service so that we tend to see health in terms of deficits or inabilities to function to our best. The glossary of health promotion however (Nutbeam 1998) defines health in positive terms as a resource for everyday life, building on the World Health Organisation definition that health is more than the absence of disease, it is a state of complete physical, mental

> **Our health services illness service so that we tend to see health in terms of deficits or inabilities to function to our best**

and social well-being (WHO 1946). By emphasising health in these positive terms and referring to social and personal resources as well as physical capabilities, health promoters offer a different perspective on inequalities in health, which can be viewed in terms of resource imbalances, rather than in disease incidence.

Reporting inequalities in health

How do we understand health inequalities in the context of rising affluence over the last fifty years? One theory is that above a base level, it is relative income rather than absolute income that is important. In this view, health depends not just on the level of your income, but where you stand in relation to others with whom you come in contact (Wilkinson and Pickett 2009).

the burden of illness falls predominantly on those at the lower end of the income scale, with people reliant on unskilled or semi-skilled employment much more likely to suffer long-term illness and to die prematurely

From the Black Report (1980) on, the tradition in discussing inequalities in health has been to show that the burden of illness falls predominantly on those at the lower end of the income scale, with people reliant on unskilled or semi-skilled employment much more likely to suffer long-term illness and to die prematurely. More recently, additional data from large-scale surveys has shown that it is these same groups who are more likely think of themselves as unhealthy, to smoke, to eat fewer fruits and vegetables and to exercise less than is recommended. These behaviours are clearly linked to their higher rates of illness and the thrust of policy has often been recent years has been to focus on altering these behaviours as a way to both improve health and reduce inequalities.

The data will be familiar to many readers, as it consistently identifies the same areas and the same social groups (Figures 1 and 2). The 2001 Census of Population, the most comprehensive source of demographic data, placed some Welsh local authorities among the most disadvantaged in the whole of the UK. In the Census, people were asked to assess their own health. Local authorities where people said they had the worst health were primarily in Wales (Merthyr Tydfil, Blaenau Gwent, Rhondda Cynon Taf, Neath Port Talbot, Caerphilly) or the north of England (National Statistics online 2010). The same local authorities also fared badly in terms of long-term limiting illness in the 2001 Census. In Merthyr Tydfil, 30 per cent of people said they had a long-term condition, and more than half of households in Merthyr Tydfil, Neath Port Talbot and Blaenau Gwent included at least one person with a limiting long-term illness.

It is these valleys that suffered in the industrial decline of South Wales, and even though they have been the target for regeneration in recent years, that legacy remains with them. It is also these areas where there are more people whose diet, weight and sedentary lifestyle might endanger their long-term health and it is also those individuals and families most likely to be affected by industrial decline: the long-term unemployed and those in routine or manual jobs who are more likely to suffer long-term illness or to smoke.

Figure 1: Percentage of adults who reported having a limiting long-term illness by socio-economic status

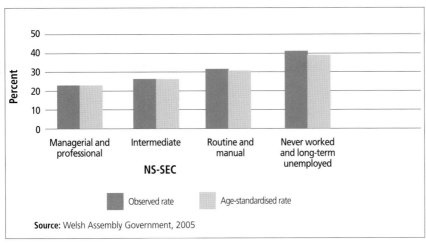

Source: Welsh Assembly Government, 2005

Figure 2: Percentage of Adults who reported being a current smoker by socio-economic status

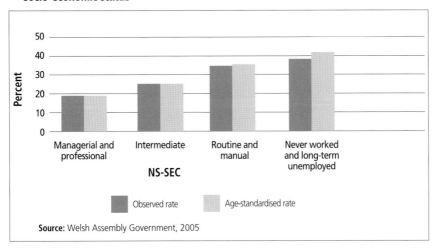

Source: Welsh Assembly Government, 2005

Health as a resource for everyday life

Remembering the health promotion definition of health as a resource for everyday life, with that positive focus, it is helpful to include in this discussion some data about what factors are related to well-being. Evidence from recent studies in the USA suggest that personal relationships are extremely important. A review of 148 separate studies (Holt-Lunstad et al 2010) concluded that the evidence was overwhelming that having good friends and strong social relationships, especially living with one or more people, improved health so dramatically that it could outweigh the impact of obesity, lack of physical activity or excessive alcohol consumption. The researchers conclude that social relationships are linked to better health practices as well as to persistent stress and depression.

Similarly, in surveys (see Figure 3), the factors affecting well-being are dominated by close personal relationships, with health and the local environment also featuring strongly.

Figure 3: Factors influencing well-being

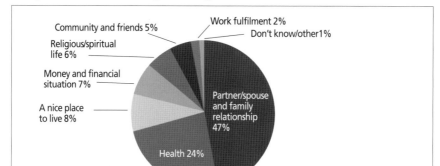

Source: Sustainable Development Commission (2009) Prosperity without Growth
www.sd-commission.org.uk/publications.php?id=914

Well-being provides a strong test of the extent to which policies are coming together to reduce inequalities and to promote sustainable development. A high-level of well-being has been noted as a feature of strong and vibrant communities (Welsh Assembly Government 2003).

The policy response

Whitehead (1998) theorises policy development as evolutionary, passing through a number of stages, from ignorance or disregard, through recognition, denial, growing awareness and measurement to the desire for action, isolated initiatives and a comprehensive policy. We can see many of these stages in the recent history of inequalities policy, from the 'samizdat' publication of the Black Report (Williams 2007) and the re-badging of inequalities as 'variations' during the Major governments; to the rise of the notions of social exclusion and joined- up government amid the initial energy and enthusiasm for change during the Blair government, to the distinctive policy directions of the Welsh Assembly Government. The appreciation of the complexity of inequalities was evident from the early days of the Blair administration – indeed, of the 39 recommendations made by the Acheson (1997) inquiry into health inequalities, only three directly concerned the NHS. This only confirmed the government view that improving the public's health and tackling inequalities needed to cross departmental boundaries (Hunter 2003) as well as reflecting MacIntyre's observation that many of the major drivers of population health and of the distribution of health lie outside the health service (McIntyre 2000).

> **many of the major drivers of population health and of the distribution of health lie outside the health service**

Following a cross-cutting review of health inequalities, then Secretary of State, Alan Milburn declared that the UK Government:

"accepts that there are wider determinants of ill health… the NHS can make a specific contribution to improving health prospects by working with the communities it serves: making the task of tackling health inequality something done with local people not just done to them… a healthier nation calls for a fairer society. The job of improving health… is a job for the whole of government – and not just between government departments but between government, business, local communities and individuals to provide real and lasting opportunities for better health."
(Milburn 2002)

Milburn's (2002) review committed the whole of government 'to *place tackling health inequalities at the very heart of public service delivery*' (Milburn 2002), while the Wanless review (Wanless 2002) considered that the future of the NHS depended on a population 'fully engaged' with its health and NHS priorities reoriented towards preventing illness. However despite this strong recommendation, broad health policy continued and continues to focus primarily on treating existing illness, rather than on upstream approaches to reducing inequalities.

The position of the current government in Westminster has been expressed by the Health Secretary Andrew Lansley who, in a speech to the Faculty of Public Health, told this expert audience that:

"…we have to change behaviour, and change people's relationships with each other and with drugs, alcohol, tobacco and food."

Not much new there then. 'Choosing Health' (2004), the previous government's public health strategy, as well as the policy of the last Conservative Government, in their 'Health of the Nation' in 1992, focused mostly on diseases and risk factors, making smoking, obesity, alcohol consumption and sexual health key indicators of progress on public health goals.

However, further into his speech, Lansley introduced a somewhat different approach, commenting that:

"social norms are much more important than policymakers have traditionally assumed. People are deeply influenced by the behaviour of those around them – and public policy should reflect that."

And he went on to talk about public health as a kind of social movement, altering the way we think about health and how to improve it. Social movements tend to be more or less informal, often grassroots organisations which form and reform, with a common purpose, often of social change. Such an idea may be compatible with new Tory notions of the 'big society', but it would be unusual for a social movement to arise out of conventional government policy processes.

While he might have wished to put clear 'blue' water between the current policy and those of the coalition's predecessors, there is a consistency in this message that continues a gradual and steady shift from the disease-focused risk factor epidemiology that characterised the 'Health of the Nation' (Department of Health 1992) to contemporary public health and health improvement policies in the twenty-first century in both the UK and Wales. Recent policy emphasises a need to engage people in health discussions as well as recognising that health is a broader issue. This incorporates, through partnerships, idea of the 'healthy public policy', and the more recent 'health in all policies' approach which systematically and explicitly includes health as a consideration for policy makers across government and is a key action in health promotion (WHO 1986; Milio 2001, Sihto et al 200).

The approach Lansley outlines in his speech echoes that of the last government in the early years of this century, when initiatives like Health Action Zones (Bauld et al 2005) and Sure Start (Melhuish 2008) focused on the materialist / structuralist explanations of ill health and inequalities (Spencer 2007), before reverting to more behaviourist models in 'Choosing Health (Department of Health 2004), although with a continued emphasis on the need to '...*shape the commercial and cultural environment...*' (Blair 2004) in order to make healthy 'choices' easier. Lansley's words show at least some appreciation of the complexity of the issue, although many would comment that it is not merely other people's behaviour that has an impact, but all of the segments in Dahlgren and Whitehead's (1992) rainbow diagram (Figure 4) of the determinants of health.

Figure 4: The Determinants of Health

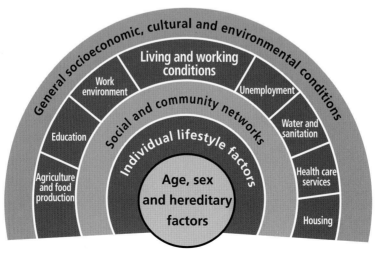

Source: Dahlgren and Whitehead 1992

The trend in the understanding of whose work can have an impact on health has been the most marked, shifting away from the pathogenic (illness focused) to the salutogenic (wellness focused). Accompanying this, particularly in Wales, is a shift from health service to local government in responsibility for health improvement. For example, the lead agencies in health and well-being partnerships are local authorities and it is local authority staff who are primarily or partly responsible for implementing public health programmes such as free swimming and healthy schools at the local level. Indeed in reporting the SHARP projects, which aimed to work with disadvantaged communities to build social capital and develop their resources, Moore (2007) found that the NHS in Wales was not always willing to participate, finding little short term benefit in such work.

In Wales, since devolution, there has been a twin focus for health and social care: on the one hand developing better services for those who need them and on the other improving the health of Welsh people (Welsh Assembly Government 2005). Along side this, the Assembly Government set out a range of commitments to reinforce their intention to development an integrated approach to policies and programmes through joint action across policy areas. 'Better Health, Better Wales' (Secretary of State for Wales 1998) was produced before devolution, but set the direction which was continued once the Assembly had been elected, strongly featuring the wider determinants of health and the importance of cross-departmental collaboration.

Soon after devolution, Professor Peter Townsend was commissioned to advise the Welsh Assembly Government on how to reallocate resources to reduce inequalities. The final report reported mortality rates in Wales to be amongst the worst in Western Europe, with heart disease and cancer rates being a major concern (Michael 2008). Rates of long-term limiting illness are also much higher in Wales than England and are particularly concentrated in the south Wales valleys, in the old coal mining and industrial areas (ONS 2003). 'Targeting Poor Health' which followed (Welsh Assembly Government 2001) emphasised issues of justice and of the wider concepts of health inequalities and has been an enduring influence on policy in Wales.

> **the emerging Welsh approach to reducing health inequalities through joint action across policy areas was in advance of most of the UK**

Subsequently, following his work for the UK Treasury, Derek Wanless headed the group which produced a 'Review of Health and Social Care in Wales' (Wanless 2004). They emphasised the importance of generating more evidence of effectiveness as well as the importance of action to prevent ill-health. The report concluded that the emerging Welsh approach to reducing health inequalities through joint action across policy areas was in advance of most of the UK. *Better Health, Better Wales* (Secretary of State for Wales 1998) had proposed promoting sustainable health and well-being, through action across government and in settings in the community.

In 2003 the Welsh Assembly Government announced funding of more than £11 million to help reduce health inequalities in Wales, targeting funding to improve access to health services for those most in need. Valleys communities in Neath Port Talbot, Rhondda Cynon Taf and Torfaen were amongst the local health boards that benefited, with initiatives supporting older people, children, and schemes targeted at mental health and coronary disease.

Before leaving the post of Chief Medical Officer for Wales, Dr Ruth Hall warned of the huge challenge ahead for public health, stating that hitherto the:

> 'sheer scale of the task to improve the health of the nation has been underestimated in Wales' .
> (Michael 2008),

Recent work at Cardiff University shows how vulnerable to the recession some communities in the valleys are, as well as illustrating their mobilisation of resources to help deal with their inequality (Elliott et al 2010).

There are also models of progress developing elsewhere. The Swedish strategy for public health (Hogstedt 2004, Marmot 2005) aims 'to create social conditions that will ensure good health for the entire population'. The eleven policy domains include five related to social determinants: participation in society, economic and social security, conditions in childhood and adolescence, healthier working life, and environment and products as well as more traditional domains related to behaviour. A recent progress report (Lundgren 2009) found that the determinants approach which focuses on structural factors in society, people's living conditions, and health behaviours that affect health was well understood and emphasizes the role of other sectors in public health. Monitoring, the participation of actors outside the health service and their understanding of the public health role were found to be crucial as was the role of government and other political bodies in promoting and coordinating action at regional and national levels. At the same time, 'new' public health workers in municipalities needed more skills development to function effectively in promoting health. A strategy to reduce 'social inequity' was introduced by the Norwegian government in 2007, with a focus on inter-sectoral efforts, the structural factors that result in health inequality, and both short and long term goals relating to the social determinants. They recognised the importance of collaboration at all levels of government from ministerial to delivery as well as the need for a long term programme and to monitor changes in health determinants, rather than health outcomes (Strand et al 2009).

> **the policy priorities to address inequalities in health have little to do with NHS services, but should focus on the impact of other sectors**

The Marmot Review in England (Marmot 2009) proposes a similar approach, directing policy towards enabling individual and community potential and placing health and sustainability in all policies. The Review concluded that the policy priorities to address inequalities in health have little to do with NHS services, but should focus on the impact of other sectors to generate better health in those most affected by inequalities.

Quantifying the cost to the country as a result of inequalities, they estimated savings on NHS treatment of about £5 billion a year, but these were far outweighed by an estimated potential for annual saving of £55-65 billion including better productivity, higher tax revenues and welfare savings.

In Wales, policy on inequalities has been diffused throughout Welsh Assembly Government policy, without yet being drawn together as a coherent whole, despite a commitment to do so by 2010 in 'Designed for Life' (2005). However the general approach, with the emphasis on structural change and the contributions from across public service accords with the Marmot and Scandinavian models.

In the USA, the Centres for Disease Control administers the REACH US programme of community action to improve health in forty centres across the country The key principles identified by the programme for effective community-level work to reduce health 'disparities' in racial and ethnic minority communities based on trust, empowerment, community participation, leadership, ownership and sustainability.

Projects are varied and adapted to their location and the ethnic group with whom they work. In Massachusetts, diabetes is known to be high among the Latino community, who also have poor access to health care. Working with local health providers and the Latino community, the program has increased uptake of retinopathy screening and treatment as well as distributing culturally competent information about diet for people who have diabetes. This represents a challenge to practice in the US, where health care and information have been restricted by ability to pay. Although disease focused, the tools that are used in the program link health to the programme priorities of empowerment, community building and sustainability. One participant said:

> "I am grateful for all you have done for me and my health. Before I began this course, my diabetes was really bad, and I was really depressed, disillusioned, and sad. With this program, I learned to be more conscientious. I feel different, better."
> (Centers for Disease Control 2007 P43)

"

health inequalities require interventions which acknowledge the complexity of the issue and work sufficiently 'upstream' to make a difference to 'downstream' indicators

Addressing inequalities: what do we know?

While descriptions of the extent of health inequalities in the UK abound, and policy advice has been relatively consistent in recent years (Department of Health 2003, Wanless 2005, McIntyre 2007, Marmot 2008, 2009), there are few evaluations of interventions designed to address inequalities and even fewer which include outcome measures (Health Development Agency 2001, Wanless 2005, MacIntyre 2007). Like other 'wicked issues' (Blackman et al 2006), health inequalities require interventions which acknowledge the complexity of the issue and work sufficiently 'upstream' to make a difference to 'downstream' indicators.

Differential health outcomes come about due to unequal access to a range of resources that support health, as well as the unequal distribution power in society, a conclusion reached by the WHO Commission on the Social Determinants of Health (2009). Attempts to address inequality have to both tackle the structures which constrain individual actions, and to build the capacity to act of those people with the least power and opportunities (Shucksmith 2000). Inequality, exclusion and marginalisation may be products of the modern world (Giddens 1991), however people, individually and collectively retain the capacity to become active agents and resist and transform their social and physical environments.

Morgan and Ziglio (2007) describe the foundation of an assets view of health in the work of Antonovsky in his development of the notion of salutogenesis, or wellness. The origin of the salutogenic theory is in interviews of Jewish women who survived the concentration camps. Antonovsky found that despite their experiences, some of the women he interviewed remained healthy and well (Eriksson 2007). The salutogenic framework can be viewed as including three dimensions, first a focus on problem solving and finding solutions, second on 'generalised resistance resources' which help people maintain health, protect against life's stresses and move them towards better health and thirdly the development of a sense of coherence which helps interpret the world as predictable, manageable and meaningful (Lindstrom & Erikkson 2006; Mosley et al 2010).

This conclusion echoes the work of Robert Putnam who in his book '*Bowling Alone*' (2000) charted the decline of community life in America over 30 years and assessed its importance. This 'social capital', which according to Putnam, refers to the features of social organization including networks, norms, and trust which facilitate coordination and cooperation for mutual benefit. Social capital can contribute considerably to the well-being of an area and enables the kind of social networking that Holt-Lunstad and her team studied. Putnam recognized that high social capital was linked with engagement in public issues, mutual trust and lawfulness, though he emphasised that both the 'bonding' capital that came from good social networks within a community and the 'bridging' capital that enabled the community to connect to wider society were necessary for positive change.

Bourdieu's version of social capital focuses on how group participation might yield individual benefits and how they build 'social capital' through social interaction. So, social capital is seen as a product of the involvement which changes relationships, into lasting obligations for example feelings of gratitude, respect and friendship (Bourdieu, 1986). This two-part definition: the social relationship which enables access to the resources of their neighbours; and the level and quality of the resources, makes us consider not only the existence of social networks in the community, its resources and individuals' abilities to make use of them, but also the unequal access that individuals and neighbourhoods have to social capital resources. And we can envisage a successful approach to tackling inequalities in health as in involving the construction of social capital through increasing the number of people active in social networks, as well as shared resources for childcare, gardening tasks, dog walking, shopping etc.

Scambler (2007) identified six possible types of assets that might be considered alongside social capital as relevant to both the existence of inequalities and their reduction. Biological and psychological assets yield the capacity to function and cope, social and cultural assets are generated through the interaction with others, special assets through the environment and material assets through the economic system. To an extent, assets may be capable of substitution, so that the notion of resilience, a psychological asset, may enable someone to cope with a poor environment or low income without an impact on health. In North West England, public health professionals have adopted an assets-based approach to tackling inequalities (IDEA 2010). Their approach strongly features participative approaches to appraisal and to building community assets. Manton in Nottingham, a former pit village, has adopted the approach through a community alliance which has aimed to rebuild social capital through empowerment. Results are encouraging with increasing involvement, trust and self-assessed health and reduced crime.

While the Putnam view may appear rose-tinted, harking back to a small town America in some mythical golden age starring James Stewart, in combination with Bourdieu and Scambler, he hints at the required complexity in addressing health inequalities, a complexity which has not to date been a feature of government policy either in the UK or Wales, but has been demonstrated in some initiatives (Cropper et al 2007; Anderson et al 2005). In the SHARP projects (Cropper et al 2007) the Welsh Assembly Government sponsored projects across the country in areas with high incidence of ill health, social exclusion and poor life chances. Each project attempted to develop and share learning though an action research approach, adding to the evidence base on partnership-driven, participative and community-based means of tackling broad social determinants of health and health inequalities. These promote a deeper understanding of the problem and long-term solutions by tracing it to its roots. However they may not provide evidence in 'traditional' forms as usually accepted by policy-makers or professionals (Carlisle et al 2007), 'wicked' issues such as health inequalities require that we take a different approach to evidence, one which accepts the ambiguities and the absence of clear and measurable indicators of outcomes.

It is only through a variety of complex and complementary strategies that public health issues can be successfully addressed. This is all the more true with regard to inequalities in health for which public health has begun to identify social processes as intervention targets (Frohlich & Potvin 2010). For example, Spencer (2007) argues that behaviours like smoking, poor nutrition and a sedentary lifestyle are not simply the result of individual choices, but are embedded in the understanding of social norms and practices and the circumstances of people's lives, influenced by their past experiences. They are the result of complex interactions between social and environmental factors and understandable if health is seen in social ecological terms. Frohlich and colleagues (2007) draw on Giddens theory of structuration (1984) to argue that tackling inequalities requires action on both structure and agency to transform people's lives. The theory contends that both agency, (that is the ability to deploy a range of capabilities and causal powers) and structure, (the rules and resources in society) result in social practices, which are the activities that make and transform the world we live in. So Frohlich argues that to succeed, tackling inequalities in health should address all of these three (agency, social structure and ultimately social practices) rather than structure or agency alone. Furthermore there is a need for the fine tuning of 'interventions' to adapt them to specific environments and moments. Reducing inequalities will require engaging with structural and environmental conditions, developing 'interventions' which alter material well-being, expectations and perceptions, in addition to acting to empower individuals and communities to enable healthy choices.

> **The benefits of addressing health inequalities would accrue throughout society, through improved productive capacity, increased tax revenues and lower welfare payments in addition to reductions in the cost of treating illness**

Health inequalities are one of the 'wicked' issues (Blackman et al 2006) that require collaboration from across society to address, so that the fundamental challenge is to involve the public, private and third sectors, at local and national level, in action as well as to develop people's individual capacity. The benefits of addressing health inequalities would accrue throughout society, through improved productive capacity, increased tax revenues and lower welfare payments in addition to reductions in the cost of treating illness. There would also be improvements in general well-being and sustainability (Marmot 2009).

Budgetary pressures, such as those we now experience, may tend to promote a risk averse culture of conservative policy-making. However creative thinking which builds on synergies between investing in sustainable communities and health will reduce inequalities and lead to benefits to the country overall. Marmot (2009) cites the example of the choice between developing parks and building roads. The roads budget could provide for a thousand new parks, providing new leisure opportunities for many and saving thousands of tons of carbon. As this suggests, tackling health inequalities requires paradigmatic shifts in thinking about how we make and deliver policy, in how we think about health and the value we place on different kinds of evidence.

In Wales, the early recognition of the importance of the social determinants of health, action to address structural issues, development of publicly funded structures to support and enable healthy choices at individual and community level provides a model for addressing health inequalities. However progress is endangered by deep cuts in social spending imposed from outside of Wales and the severity of the economic downturn, which threaten to have the greatest impact in the very areas where health status is already poor, inequalities most evident and which have never recovered from previous economic downturns.

Michael Shepherd is Senior Research Fellow at the Cardiff Institute for Society, Health and Ethics, Cardiff University

References

Anderson, E., Shepherd, M., Salisbury, C. (2006) ' "Taking off the suit": engaging the community in primary health care decision-making'. *Health Expectations*, 9(1), 70-80

Bauld, L., Benzeval, M., Judge, K., Mackinnon, J., Sullivan, H. (2005) 'Assessing the Impact of Health Action Zones', in Barnes, M., Bauld, L., Benzeval, M., Judge, K., Mackenzie, M. and Sullivan, H. (Eds.) *Health Action Zones: Partnerships for Health Equity*. Routledge: Abingdon

BBC News (2010) http://www.bbc.co.uk/news/health-10730095 Accessed 9.8.10

Bennett, K., Beynon, H. and Hudson, R. (2000) *Coalfields regeneration: dealing with the consequences of industrial decline*. Joseph Rowntree Foundation: York

Black, D. (1980) *Inequalities in Health: Report of a Research Working Group* (The Black Report). DHSS: London

Blackman, T., Elliott, E., Greene, A., Harrington, B., Hunter, D., Marks, L., McKee, L. and Williams, G. (2006), 'Performance assessment and wicked problems: the case of health inequalities', *Public Policy and Administration*, Vol. 21 No.2, 66-80.

Blair, T. (2004) Foreword to *Choosing Health*. Department of Health: London

Bourdieu, P. (1986) 'The forms of capital', in Richardson, J. (Ed.) *Handbook of Theory and Research for the Sociology of Education*. Greenwood: New York

Carlisle, S., Snooks, H., Evans, A. and Cohen, D. (2007) 'Evaluation, evidence and learning in community-based action research', in Cropper, S., Porter, A., Williams, G., Carlisle, S., Moore, R., O'Neill, M., Roberts, C. and Snooks, H. (eds) *Community Health & Wellbeing*. Policy Press: Bristol

Centers for Disease Control and Prevention (2007) The Power to Reduce Health Disparities: Voices from REACH Communities. U.S. Department of Health and Human Services, Centers for Disease Control and Prevention: Atlanta

Cropper, S., Porter, A., Williams, G., Carlisle, S., Moore, R., O'Neill, M., Roberts, C. and Snooks, H. (eds) Community Health & Wellbeing. Policy Press: Bristol

Dahlgren, G. and Whitehead, M. (1992) *Policies and strategies to promote social equity in health*. World Health Organization: Copenhagen

Department of Health (2004) *Choosing Health: Making healthier Choices Easier.* DoH: London

Elliott, E., Harrop, E., Rothwell, H., Shepherd, M., and Williams, G. H. (2010). *The impact of the economic downturn on health in Wales: A review and case study.* Welsh Health Impact Assessment Support Unit: Cardiff.

Erikkson, M. (2007) *Unravelling the mystery of salutogenesis*. Folkhalsan Research Centre: Helsinki

Frohlich, K.L. and Potvin, L. (2010) 'Commentary: structure or agency? The importance of both for addressing social inequalities in health'. Int J Epidemiol. 39(2): 78-9.

Frohlich,K. Dunn,J., McLaren, L., Shiell, A., Potvin, L., Hawe, P., Dass, C. and Thurston, W. (2007) 'Understanding place and health: A heuristic for using administrative data'. *Health & Place* 13, 2, 299-309

Giddens, A. (1984) *The constitution of society.* Polity Press: Cambridge

Giddens, A. (1991) *Modernity and self-identity.* Polity Press: Cambridge

Hogstedt, H., Lundgren, B., Moberg, H., Pettersson, B. and Agren, G. (2004) 'The Swedish public health policy and the National Institute of Public Health', *Scan J Public Health* 32 (suppl 64), 1–64.

Holt-Lunstad, J., Smith, T.B., Layton, J.B. (2010) 'Social Relationships and Mortality Risk: A Meta-analytic Review'. *PLoS* Med 7(7): e1000316. doi:10.1371/journal.pmed.1000316

Hunter, D.J. (2003) Public Health Policy. Polity Press: Oxford

IDEA (2010) A glass half-full: how an asset approach can improve community health and well-being. http://www.idea.gov.uk/idk/aio/18410498 Accessed 14/09/2010

Lansley, A. (2010) *A new approach to public health.* http://www.dh.gov.uk/en/MediaCentre/Speeches/DH_117280 Accessed August 19, 2010

Lindstrom, B. & Erikkson, M. (2006) 'Contextualising salutogenesis and Antonovsky in public health development'. *Health Promotion International* 21, 3, 238-244

Marmot, M. (2005) 'Social determinants of health inequalities', *Lancet*, 365, 9464, 1099-1104

Melhuish, E., Belsky, J., Leyland, A.H. and Barnes, J. (2008) 'Effects of fully-established Sure Start Local Programmes on 3-year-old children and their families living in England: a quasi-experimental observational study'. *Lancet* 372, 9560, 1641-1647

Michael, P. (2008) *Public Health in Wales (1800-2000) – a brief history.* Welsh Assembly Government: Cardiff

Milburn, A. (2002) Speech by Alan Milburn to the Faculty of Public Health Medicine, 20 November 2002

Milio, N. (1987) 'Making healthy public policy: developing the science by learning the art: an ecological framework for policy studies'. *Health Promot. Int.* 2: 263-274

Milio, N. (2001) 'Glossary: healthy public policy'. *Journal of Epidemiology and Community Health 55*, (9) (September 1): 622–623.

Moore, R. (2007) 'Social theory, social policy and sustainable communities', in Cropper, S., Porter, A., Williams, G., Carlisle, S., Moore, R., O'Neill, M., Roberts, C., and Snooks, H. (eds) *Community Health & Wellbeing.* Policy Press: Bristol

Morgan, A. & Ziglio, E. (2007) 'Revitalising the evidence base for public health: an assets model', *Promotion and Education Supplement* 2 pp17-22

Mosley, P., Eriksson, M., Lindstrom, B. and Sagy, S. (2010) *Family sense of coherence and connectedness.* Poster at IUHPE World Conference, Geneva 2010.

National Statistics online (2010) http://www.statistics.gov.uk/cci/nugget.asp?id=916 accessed 27.8.10

National Statistics online (2010) http://www.statistics.gov.uk/census2001/profiles/commentaries/health.asp#illness accessed 27.8.10

Nutbeam, D. (1998). Health Promotion Glossary. *Health Promotion International*, 13,4 349-364

Putnam, R. (2000) *Bowling Alone: the collapse and revival of American Community.* Simon & Schuster: New York

Scambler, G. (2007) 'Social structure and the production, reproduction and durability of health inequalities'. *Social Theory and Health*, 5, 297-315.

Secretary of State for Wales (1998) *Better Health, Better Wales.* HMSO: Cardiff

Shucksmith, M. (2000) 'Endogenous Development, Social Capital and Social Inclusion: perspectives from leader in the UK'. *Sociologia Ruralis*, 40(2), 208-218

Sihto, M., Ollila, E. and Koivusalo, M. (2006) Principles and challenges of Health in all Policies: Prospects and Potentials, in Ståhl, T., Wismar, M., Ollila, E., Lahtinen, E. and Leppo, K. (eds) Ministry of Social Affairs and Health/European Observatory on Health Systems and Policies: Helsinki

Spencer, N. (2007) 'Behaving badly? Smoking and the role of behaviour chance in tackling health inequalities', in Dowler, E. and Spencer, N. (eds) *Challenging Health inequalities: from Acheson to Choosing Health.* Policy Press: Bristol.

Strand, M., Brown, C., Torgerson, T. and Giaever, O. (2009) 'Setting the political agenda to tackle health inequity in Norway'. *Studies on social and economic determinants of population health No 4.* WHO Europe: Copenhagen

Thomas, B., Dorling, D., Davey Smith, G. (2010) 'Inequalities in premature mortality in Britain: observational study from 1921 to 2007', *BMJ*, 341:c3639

Wanless, D. (2002) *The Wanless Report.* HM Treasury: London

Wanless, D. (2004) *Review of Health and Social Care in Wales,* Welsh Assembly Government: Cardiff

Welsh Assembly Government (2001) 'Well Being in Wales' http://www.cmo.wales.gov.uk/content/work/well-being-in-wales/consultation-document-e.pdf

Welsh Assembly Government (2005) Welsh Health Survey 2004/05 http://new.wales.gov.uk/cisd/publications/statspubs/healthsurv200405/docen.pdf?lang=en Accessed 9.8.10

Whitehead, M. (1998) 'Diffusion of ideas on social inequalities in health: a European perspective'. *Milbank Quarterly* 76(2) 469-492

Wilkinson, R. and Pickett, K. (2009) *The Spirit Level: Why more equal societies almost always do better.* Allen Lane: London

Williams, G. (2007) 'Health inequalities in their place', in Cropper, S., Porter, A., Williams, G., Carlisle, S., Moore, R., O'Neill, M., Roberts, C., and Snooks, H. (eds) *Community Health & Wellbeing.* Policy Press: Bristol

World Health Organisation (WHO) (1946) *Preamble to the Constitution of the World Health Organization as adopted by the International Health Conference,* New York, 19-22 June, 1946

World Health Organisation (1986) The Ottawa Charter of Health Promotion. Health Promotion, 1, i-v [http://metalib.cf.ac.uk:8331/INS01/icon_eng/v-sfx-1.gif]

A lone voice
struggling to be heard

*Ida's story*_____

"My husband had a severe stroke when we were starting a walking holiday in Scotland. He spent two weeks in (name of Scottish hospital withheld) where speech and physiotherapy were begun almost immediately and the consultant sought me out daily to explain and give what help he could. My husband was transferred to (name of Welsh hospital withheld) because the website claimed it had a stroke unit. This was not true and, on arrival, after an exhausting journey by ambulance, he was put on a general medical ward. There seemed to be no concept that prompt treatment was necessary, even the bed was unsuitable. No speech – or physiotherapy was forthcoming, until I insisted on it. My husband, unable to stand unaided, unable to use his right hand or arm, unable to speak, obviously thought he had been sent there to die. And indeed, that ward was a grim place. We battled to get him transferred to (name of rehabilitation ward withheld). Even in this ward the care was patchy, some wonderful nurses, some very off-hand. I made a formal complaint about one who drained my husband's drip into his drinking cup and then reconnected it. I learnt later that another patient's wife complained about her because she changed three patient's catheters without changing her gloves. She was a ward sister. My husband then developed pneumonia despite the fact that several visitors had reported his deteriorating condition at the nurses' desk for five days beforehand. The consultant was difficult to contact and patronising in the extreme. It was obvious to me that my husband was 66 years old and not considered worthy of much care. This was a shock to us because we led very active lives til the day of my husband's stroke and never considered ourselves old. We walked a lot, fell walking, not country strolls. I had never realised how universal was that dismissive attitude to people in their 60s. I have since discovered that it's true in local and national government as well.

My husband was discharged after seven and a half months. I wasn't given a copy of his discharge notes. As we'd had very little to do with hospitals before I didn't even know these things existed and nobody told me he'd been having epileptic fits while in hospital. The first fit at home was, therefore, a tremendous shock.

We were offered all sorts of information, an over-whelming amount. Every agency, physio, speech therapist, this and that clinic seemed to demand our undivided attention. Acronyms came thick and fast. They obviously meant something to those who used them, but how were we supposed to understand them? You really cannot concentrate at a time like this. I still have trouble concentrating. I am tired all the time and there are so many things to be responsible for. My husband's medication is a big responsibility and I'm tired of being sent a week's supply when I ask for a repeat prescription.

> **Acronyms came thick and fast**

An occupational therapist came. She was very young and very tactless. "That'll have to go," she said disdainfully, indicating a round rug on our polished floor, "And that'll have to go," she said again of a small bookcase in the hallway. I didn't reply because I was upset at her attitude. The rug had taken months to track down.

We have an excellent social worker. Without her I don't know how we would have got through the morass of information and misinformation in which we found ourselves. This was a completely alien world. People said, "Take whatever help you can get." "You can get a grant for this and that." "You'll get mobility allowance and carer's allowance" and so on. This was well meaning but mostly inaccurate, and it all raised false hopes. It was a tiring, frustrating time. I made moves to sort things out, only to be told in the end that we didn't qualify for any financial aid except Attendance Allowance. The reason – John was 66 when he had his stroke. Had it been 18 months earlier he could have claimed mobility allowance for the rest of his life. Where's the justice or logic in that? If you've paid into the system all your life why can't you get help from it when you need it?

We had to pay for a powered wheelchair: £2,000. There was a long wait, up to two years for an NHS one, and I could not manage with the house wheelchair when we had hospital, doctor's or dentist's appointments. Then we needed a car that would accommodate the wheelchair complete with occupant. This had to be adapted.

The bathroom had to be extended. The council provided an architect to draw up the plans and the VAT was waived. Other than that all the cost was ours: over £20,000. There are so many extra costs now. I have accepted that my husband needs carers to help him get up in the morning. The authority has decreed that he needs two carers and their hourly rate goes up every year. It is now £15.28 an hour. How can authorities, local and national, say they are encouraging people to care for disabled people at home when they make it so difficult and so costly?

To move my husband we have to use a gadget called a rotunda. It is an ungainly object which I alternately bless and curse. Without it we really would be in trouble. It is a metal disc which lies on the ground and it has a handle which sticks up about four and a half feet. I manoeuvre the disc under John's feet as he sits and he pulls himself up to standing. The rotunda not surprisingly turns round on its base and John can then lower himself down into the next chair which I will have positioned. This exercise, such as it is, is good for him and more dignified than using a hoist. When the rotunda was first delivered, the OT said, "You'll be able to take it with you when you go to the supermarket and things." Yes, right, 12 kilos of awkwardly shaped metal. Do they know what they're saying?

Carers, from Council or agency, vary enormously. We have had very good ones and very poor ones. With one agency John had 14 carers in 12 months. Things that upset me include:

1. Paid carers being careless with the house and furniture. It's a regular thing to have to sweep up white paint from skirting boards and radiators.

2. Picking up whatever towel comes to hand to dry John. His towels are kept over the bathroom radiator to be warm for him.

3. Talking to each other the whole time. My husband struggles to communicate but he knows what he wants to say. He's an intelligent man being ignored.

4. Talking to him as if he's a slow-witted three-year old.

I could continue. The first two probably sound petty but life is made up of small things and we spend more time at home now so I guess this thing matters more than it did.

The worst single aspect of John's disability is his dysphasia. He used to explain complex concepts to students. Now he can't ask for a cup of tea without prompting. This is not because he is no longer intelligent. It's not a matter of re-learning words. The centre of the brain, which learnt them when John was a child, is damaged. Sometimes John wants something and we spend 20 minutes trying to ascertain what it is. Can you imagine how frustrating this must be? Sometimes when we're with friends and someone can't quite remember a detail of something that was on the news or in a film, we can see that John knows it, but he can't tell us. Can you imagine what it's like to be in a strange environment and unable to explain what you need?

Incorrect invoices for carers' services have caused me a great deal of worry and distress. There have been more incorrect invoices than correct ones over the three and a half years that carers have been coming to help us. The first time it happened I rang up to say that the bill was too low, that we must have someone else's bill. The next thing I heard was a letter from the debtor's department to say that payment for the original bill was overdue. How could this be? I hadn't yet received the correct invoice. I was very upset. Nobody has ever accused us of owing anything before. I also wondered, and still do, what happens to people too confused to query their bills.

They mean well but you do feel you no longer exist.

Caring is a very lonely occupation. People are wary of disturbing you in case you are busy with your charge, though official bodies seem to think you're waiting in with bated breath for them to call. You are lonely also because friends move on. I don't mean they lose touch entirely, but I can no longer attend MU (Mothers' Union) meetings. They take place in the evenings and my evenings are fully occupied with making tea and getting John ready for bed. I couldn't face coming in at 9.30pm and starting the routine then, even if I could get someone to stay with John in my absence.

The MU day outings are even less feasible. Friends naturally continue their active membership, one more thing we no longer have in common. I used to be a member of a church quiz team. We only quizzed once a year in an inter-church quiz to raise money for charity. After John's stroke I wasn't asked to participate. I know I couldn't and I know they realised that, but it hurt not to be asked again. We couldn't make it to two Ruby weddings last year because we couldn't get the wheelchair into the venues. People continually say things like, "I didn't ask you to come because I knew you wouldn't be able to make it." They mean well but you do feel you no longer exist.

You feel you are a lone voice struggling to be heard. You feel that officials really would like you to go away and not bother them. You feel that you are being milked of your savings. You feel you have so much to be responsible for, yet you have little control over your life.

Written by Ida Turley,
and compiled by Disability Wales.

Speaking
Naomi's language

*Naomi's (and her family's) story*_____

Naomi first came to Touch Trust five
years ago. Touch Trust is dedicated to
delivering its unique therapy
programme to individuals and groups
with complex needs.

"The position of Touch Trust at the heart of the Wales Millennium Centre is
almost as important as what Touch Trust gives its guests. That it should
inhabit a Centre intended to be a national monument to art and music
only confirms its role as a leading light in the education of people with
extremely complex special needs.

The Touch Trust space stands proud, trumpeting its role as one of the most
important events that has happened to the people for whom its welcome
is like a divine blessing.

The people who deliver this most subtle of holistic programmes can have
no idea what they give to their guests and their families, some of whom
have spent many lonely hours in the corridors of clinics housed in back-
street buildings, like a carelessly attired and inconvenient old aunt,
waiting to hear quietly delivered messages of despair –"don't expect
much, don't try, don't hope.

The Touch Trust team are not familiar with "don't". The space reflects the
people who made it, bright and full of positive energy. For those of us
who have fought our way through a mish-mash of badly under-resourced
government provision for our relatives, walking through Touch Trust's
doors has been much like leaving the real world of frustration and
struggle behind, and finding ourselves in a kind of Paradise.

The first time I went to a Touch Trust session with my sister, I was shocked
by the effusive greeting we received, having become accustomed to
horrified gaping at her dis-inhibited behaviours, and the distance this set
between us and the rest of humanity. Dilys and Charlotte seemed to
accept these things as aspects of her personality, just as if she were shy or
aloof. On reflection, it speaks volumes about how isolated we had

become in terms of social interaction, that the fact of this attitude could elicit such a response.

The session proceeded to entertain me for its unfamiliar joviality and celebration of Naomi and her eccentricities. I left feeling suffused with optimism and the sense that a better world awaited us. And so it did.

Since that day, some years ago now, Naomi has benefited substantially from the unique approach of Touch Trust. This means that, as a consequence, my family and I have benefited, not only personally from accompanying Naomi to her sessions but also from the positive effects of attendance on her psychological state and behaviour.

> **I left feeling suffused with optimism and the sense that a better world awaited us**

It is not over-stating the case to say that Touch Trust is essential to people like my little sister and me and my family. I feel so lucky to be able to attend her sessions with her, and am humbled every time I am there to meet the people Dilys has chosen to be on her team. People like Dave, who doesn't question the peculiar roles he is asked to assume to enable the guests to showcase their work (as when he is a cheerful octopus in a "sharing and showing performance" on Glanfa stage), or Emily, who approaches her work as if it were one continuous party. I have also been lucky enough to meet some of the trustees, who speak of being "Dilysed" which I suspect is a term which will soon enough turn up in the OED.

The power of Dilys's idea has meant more to us than any Act of Parliament to outlaw discrimination, or any government target concerning state-provided services.

Touch Trust speaks Naomi's language, which is music and other noise, and the Trust allows her space to find a way to make that noise a tool to express herself in a meaningful way. She has learnt how to tolerate invasions of her personal space which had previously elicited violent tantrums, and how to be quiet for others to have their say (sometimes!).

The only sadness I feel in respect of Touch Trust is that it is not more widely available so that other families who face the same rock face that we did can feel that same sense of homecoming and freedom to be the family they should be.

Written by Claire Perkins, a member of Naomi's family, and compiled by the Touch Trust

6.

MATERIAL
POVERTY
and
Social
Exclusion

Financial
exclusion

Lindsey Kearton

FINANCIAL EXCLUSION IS GENERALLY defined as the inability, reluctance or difficulty of particular groups of consumers to access mainstream financial products and services. It also relates to a person's financial capability i.e. the knowledge and skills they have to make confident and informed financial decisions.

For most people having a bank account is part of everyday life. There is no need to carry much cash around as the majority of things are paid for with a debit card and many household bills are covered by monthly direct debit payments. If they need cash, they can generally access it readily at any number of free-to-use ATMs or by using the cash-back facility on their debit card. The times when people may need a little extra help financially are covered by access to an agreed overdraft facility with their bank or building society, or they may choose to take out a personal loan or use a credit card. Having a bank account also enables people to take advantage of on-line deals and to spread the cost of buying certain, more costly items, such as furniture, large electrical goods and insurance, over several months if they so wish, making them generally more affordable.

However the situation is very different for people with limited or no interaction with financial products or services, many of whom will already be living on a low or limited income. More often than not people without bank accounts, those who prefer to manage their budgets in cash, or those who are denied access to mainstream credit facilities will end up paying more to furnish their home, more to borrow money for unexpected events and emergencies, and more to access their cash because they have to rely on expensive cheque-cashing facilities (this can often be more than 10 per cent of the value of the cheque) or travel further to find a free-to-use ATM.

> **people without bank accounts, those who prefer to manage their budgets in cash, or those who are denied access to mainstream credit facilities will end up paying more**

In addition a lack of knowledge and understanding of money issues can frequently lead people to make poor financial decisions, the unintentional consequences of which can result in the purchase or use of more costly, inappropriate or unnecessary financial products, difficulties in budgeting, and being more prone to unmanageable debt and exploitation from unscrupulous financial providers. The costs people on lower incomes have to bear to gain access to cash and credit, and pay for essential goods and services are frequently described as the 'poverty premium'. Work undertaken by Save the Children and the Family Welfare Association in 2007 estimated the value of the 'poverty premium' to be around £1,000 a year.

Being financially excluded often impacts on many other areas of people's lives frequently limiting their life choices and opportunities. People who are financially excluded are also more likely to be living in poverty, be fuel poor and suffer from poor health.

Although there are exceptions, in general vulnerability to financial exclusion is strongly correlated with low income. Low income is often a common denominator for many groups disproportionally represented amongst the financially excluded including lone parents, social housing tenants, some minority ethnic groups, people with mental health conditions, people who have a long-term illness or disability, young people and pensioners.

What causes financial exclusion?

There have been considerable changes in the financial services sector over the last twenty years. The de-regulation of the financial services industry in the 1980s helped prompt the proliferation of financial products and services we now have today. While for some consumers this has brought greater choice and opportunity to shop around for the best deals, as previously mentioned many consumers in Wales remain without even the most basic financial products or they lack the skills and confidence needed to make the right choices.

People's ability to access financial products and services is dictated by a complex range of factors. Being in close proximity to a bank, building society, post office or cash machine is just one element – often exclusion goes far beyond physical access. The way services are delivered and the suitability of the product to people's needs and circumstances are equally critical, as are overcoming institutional barriers (i.e. being refused a bank account or turned down for credit) and changing the long-established behaviours of financially excluded individuals.

Paying by cash was an active choice for the majority of consumers

Recent research by Consumer Focus Wales[1] helped to paint the picture of the everyday experiences of low-income families who live on the edge of financial inclusion, largely living on cash budgets. It also highlighted the complexities that surround low-income consumers' interaction with financial products and services. In some areas, most notably bank accounts, self-exclusion was commonplace when it came to using accounts to their full potential. Paying by cash was an active choice for the majority of consumers in the study and not just a default position. The realities of having to live on a low income meant most had a very 'sensible' attitude to money management. The need to maintain control over their finances, a general aversion to going into debt, and feelings of trust (or mistrust) towards different financial services providers were all key drivers for choosing to use cash. However more critically in other areas, such as accessing reasonably-priced credit, a sense of enforced exclusion was evident. Affordability was also a real issue when it came to taking out insurance or building up savings.

In addition, recent changes in government policy and advances in technology are helping to drive changes on how we all manage our finances and pay for goods and services. Each new development has implications for the financial inclusion agenda. Examples include the direct payment of benefits, people having to take greater responsibility for their long-term financial future, the demise of cheques and the growth of on-line banking.

> **the recent economic crisis is already hitting many consumers in Wales hard. Almost half the adult population is finding it harder to manage financially now compared to a year ago**

More recent research shows the recent economic crisis is already hitting many consumers in Wales hard. Almost half the adult population is finding it harder to manage financially now compared to a year ago, with a quarter predicting their financial situation will get worse over the next 12 months.[2]

The general rise in the cost of living and Government plans to reduce the deficit, including public sector cutbacks, benefit and tax credit changes, and an increasing likelihood of redundancies, mean pressures on household finances are set to continue over the next couple of years. This will only serve to exacerbate the need for people to have access to appropriate support and be better informed on money issues.

What is being done to address financial exclusion?

There have been a number of positive developments in recent years to promote financial inclusion amongst the population of Wales, both at the Wales and UK level. The Welsh Assembly Government's financial inclusion strategy *'Taking everyone into account'* (July 2009) has helped to provide a much needed focus and direction for this work.

The UK Government's £250 million dedicated Financial Inclusion Fund (FIF), which is now in its second phase (2008-2011), has also helped to fund several key initiatives in Wales since it was first set-up in 2004 including:

- the face-to-face debt advice project (jointly run by Citizens Advice Cymru and Shelter Cymru), which currently funds an additional 36 specialist debt advisers across Wales;
- the Department for Work and Pensions (DWP) Growth Fund, which was set-up to increase the availability of affordable loans via the third sector. As of September 2009 over 9,500 loans have been made in Wales with the help of the Growth Fund;
- the joint DWP/Treasury Financial Inclusion Champions Initiative which aims to promote all aspects of financial inclusion with a particular focus on building stronger partnerships at the local/community level. The Welsh Assembly Government also part funds the team in Wales.

Other UK-wide initiatives include the setting up of an All-Wales Illegal Money Lending Unit (funded by the UK Government since the end of 2007); the LINK 'free-to-use' ATM programme to promote access to free cash machines in deprived communities; and the Office of Fair Trading 'Save Xmas' campaign launched in June 2007 in the aftermath of the Farepak collapse.

There has also been substantial progress in the promotion of financial capability. The Consumer Financial Education Body (CFEB), established in April 2010, is continuing to deliver a range of financial capability programmes and resources across Wales as part of the Financial Services Authority (FSA) National Financial Capability Strategy. These include workplace seminars; work with universities and further education colleges; the '*Parents Guide to Money*'; work with young people not in education, employment or training; as well as work with offenders; people with mental health conditions and people facing redundancy.

More recently the provision of generic financial advice is being promoted via the CFEB '*Moneymadeclear*' service – currently available on-line and over the telephone and soon to be available face-to-face across Wales from spring 2011. Citizens Advice Bureaux also continue to be one of the key deliverers of face-to-face financial literacy advice to consumers in Wales. During 2008/09 over half of all bureaux in England and Wales provided financial capability services within their local communities as part of the Citizens Advice *Financial Skills for Life* programme.

the current climate for organisations delivering financial inclusion work is an uncertain one

However the current climate for organisations delivering financial inclusion work is an uncertain one. While there are many examples of successful financial inclusion projects and partnerships delivering work across Wales the impact of government spending cuts and changing agendas raise fundamental questions about the future of this work and how best it can be continued.

A number of key funding streams from the UK Government, including the FIF, are due to come to an end in spring 2011 with no alternatives currently in sight. Other initiatives originally set-up or proposed by the last Government, such as the Child Trust Fund (CTF) and the Savings Gateway[3], are being phased out or cancelled. Asset-based welfare programmes such as these have generally been viewed very positively by the Welsh Assembly Government. Both the Savings Gateway and the CTF were seen as important programmes for helping to tackle child poverty and financial exclusion in the medium and longer term by encouraging formal saving amongst consumers in Wales, particularly amongst low-income households. They were also regarded as key ways to increase credit union membership. Now they're being phased out or not even started (in the case of the Savings Gateway) the Welsh Assembly Government will need to find additional ways of taking this work forward.

On a positive note, the Coalition Government has committed to rolling out the CFEB-led National Financial Advice Service (the face-to-face element of '*Moneymadeclear*'); expressed a commitment to develop the credit union movement, and shown support for developing the provision of financial services through the Post Office network.

In terms of the work that has been done to date, while we have seen some progress in tackling financial exclusion over recent years, considerable challenges remain. Developing financial products and services that are better suited to the needs and circumstances of low income consumers is a critical part of the financial inclusion agenda. There are now a range of products available that have been designed to help satisfy these needs – basic bank accounts, credit union current accounts and loans, and insurance with-rent schemes to name but a few. However each of these products has experienced varying levels of success both in terms of take-up and levels of usage.

The reasons behind this are many and varied but there are indications that some of these products may not be fully meeting consumer needs. For example although the proportion of unbanked individuals has reduced, many low-income consumers are still reluctant to make full use of having a bank account. So long as banks continue to use punitive bank charges this situation is unlikely to improve.

> **although the proportion of unbanked individuals has reduced, many low-income consumers are still reluctant to make full use of having a bank account**

For other products or services, such as credit unions and insurance with-rent schemes, there appears to be a lack of understanding of how they work or a general lack of awareness that they even exist. Credit unions form an integral part of the Welsh Assembly Government's financial inclusion policy and as a result have received considerable financial support from Welsh Assembly Government and European funding over the last ten years. In spite of the fact there is now all-Wales coverage and credit union membership has increased during this time, currently less than 2 per cent of the population in Wales are members of a credit union.

Many low-income households still feel they have little choice but to turn to high cost lenders in order to help make ends meet or cope with any unexpected expenses they may face. Breaking this reliance on the high cost credit sector remains a major challenge. The challenge for third sector lenders may be considerable but equally there has probably never been a better time for them to capitalise on the evident interest and growing need for their services. The current financial climate offers significant opportunities to boost the role of community banking in Wales. The Welsh Assembly Government have recently committed to supporting the credit union movement in Wales over the next three years. Building sustainability into alternative lending approaches, such as credit unions and Community Development Finance Institutions (CDFIs), and developing the capacity of these organisations and other trusted providers, such as the Post Office, to offer additional financial services will be critical if they are to continue to provide affordable small-scale loans, savings facilities and other financial products that are more appropriate to the needs and circumstances of people living on a low income.

In addition to addressing consumer concerns about certain products and raising awareness of less costly alternatives, progress in reducing financial exclusion could also be improved by having a better understanding of what influences financial behaviours.

Conclusion

> **a financially inclusive society is a key element of the social inclusion agenda...**

Developing a financially inclusive society is a key element of the social inclusion agenda but it is also critical that action to tackle financial exclusion is not disconnected from work being taken forward in other areas. Financial exclusion can inhibit the effective delivery of many government policies including neighbourhood renewal strategies, the eradication of child poverty and fuel poverty, as well as action to improve health and well being, digital inclusion, and the improvement of public services. As a consequence efforts to tackle it need to be embedded into policy programmes across local and national government so that resources can be targeted effectively and support reaches those most in need.

There is no doubt these are tough times. Cutbacks and consolidation in frontline support services and community-based programmes may be inevitable and necessary. At the same time, there has also never been a more important time for the work on financial inclusion to continue with demand for many of these services, such as debt advice and the need for affordable loans, set to escalate.

Over the coming months it will be vital that the impact of the work that has been done to date to promote financial inclusion is not lost and that any cutback in spending is carefully managed to avoid many consumers in Wales facing additional exclusion, disadvantage and hardship at a time when they are most likely to need support.

Lindsey Kearton is Senior Policy Advocate at Consumer Focus Wales

Notes
1 'Consumer Focus Wales (2009) The cost of cash.
2 Consumer Focus Wales (2010) 'Consumer finances in Wales: debt and credit use'.
3 A Government-supported cash savings scheme to encourage working age people on lower incomes to start saving small amounts of money.

Fuel poverty in Wales

James Radcliffe

THE WINTER OF 2009/10 was one of the coldest winters in recent years, with many local authorities struggling to cope with the need to maintain roads and services through an unexpectedly cold winter. The cold weather brought to the surface many issues regarding the ability of the UK to cope with extreme temperatures.[1] One of those issues is fuel poverty, with the excess death rate in the UK during the winter higher than in other European countries with similar winter climates.[2]

Fuel poverty is usually defined as households who need to spend 10 per cent or more of their income to maintain an adequate level of heating. So a household with an annual income of £10,000 is in fuel poverty if it would be required to spend over £1,000 on maintaining adequate warmth – which is defined by the World Health Organisation as 21C in the living room, and 18C in the other rooms. It is worth noting that just because a household needs to spend 10 per cent of its income to heat their home adequately, it doesn't mean that they actually do. This is an important point to consider as we examine the issue of fuel poverty further on.

Incidence of fuel poverty

Estimates of fuel poverty in Wales in the 1990s indicated that there were 220,000 households in Wales suffering from fuel poverty. This was an estimate produced using eligibility for the Home Energy Efficiency Scheme (HEES). Subsequently, more detailed analysis found this to be an underestimate of the scale of the problem, and that the real figure was more likely to be around 360,000 households. A combination of increased incomes and lower energy prices in subsequent years saw the number of households in fuel poverty drop to between 134,000 households and 167,000 households depending on whether 'net' or 'disposable' income was used (11 to 14 per cent of households).[3] Fuel poverty was found to be particularly concentrated amongst vulnerable households (defined as those households with a member aged 60 or over, with any dependent children aged under 16 or with any long-term sick or disabled member), with 86 per cent of fuel poor households containing a vulnerable person.

> **Fuel poverty was particularly concentrated amongst vulnerable households**

Analysis by Gordon and Fahmy[4] found that there are significant predictors of fuel poverty: (1) Households where the main person is unemployed or economically inactive; (2) households lacking basic facilities such as central heating; (3) single person, single pensioner or lone-parent households; (4)

Under-occupied households (where 1 person lives in a place with 5 or more rooms); and (5) households living in properties built before 1914. The analysis also indicates that fuel poverty is far more prevalent in rural areas of Wales and the South Wales Valleys than in urban centres such as Cardiff and Swansea. Fuel poverty in Wales is higher than in England, and this is explained by a combination of poorer housing stock and higher fuel prices.

Causes of fuel poverty

The crucial factor that determines whether a household is in fuel poverty is the relationship between the income of that household and the cost of the fuel needed to maintain an adequate heat in the household.

Households that are in fuel poverty tend to be those that have a low household income, and/or live in homes that are energy inefficient. Energy prices are also an extremely important factor. There may be other factors that increase a household's fuel consumption, such as a household member having a health condition that means they need a higher than normal level of warmth.

The reasons why some households have low incomes are obvious. The most common reason is that a household contains nobody in full-time employment. This could be because the occupants are on out-of-work benefits, only work part-time, or are retired on a low income. A further cause could be if the household suffers an 'economic shock' like the loss of a job, or diagnosis of a serious illness. Household incomes are thus related to wider trends such as the performance of the economy, and the value of certain benefits such as pensions and disability-related benefits.

Housing characteristics are also an important factor in fuel poverty, because they essentially determine how much energy is required to maintain an adequate heat and what energy is available. Older houses tend to be less energy efficient than new build homes whilst the location of housing can also determine what kinds of fuel can be used. For example: a significant number of houses in Wales are in rural areas without access to the gas network, the cheapest form of heating.

The other major factor that affects fuel poverty is the price of fuel. In Wales, energy bills are generally higher than in England. Consumer Focus Wales notes:

"The average electricity consumer in south Wales pays £467 a year compared to an average of £433 in the English Midlands, a difference of £34. The annual average in north Wales is £455 compared to £427 in North West England, a difference of £28."[5]

Within Wales there are further regional divides with fuel bills in more rural areas of Wales generally higher than in urban areas. These differences are attributed to the increased costs of distributing electricity from power stations to homes. The method of payment chosen by consumers in Wales is also significant. There are savings to be made if somebody switches to direct debit and/or duel fuel deals, and considerable savings to be made if somebody switches to online methods of payment.[6] However 18 per cent of consumers in Wales use pre-payment meters, and a quarter of households pay for their gas and electricity via 'monthly/quarterly billing' (24 per cent).[7]

A further reason for higher prices in Wales is the fact that levels of switching between suppliers are low. South Wales in particular has an unusually high level of people who have remained with their original supplier.[8]

Energy prices themselves have also changed over time, and have affected the levels of fuel poverty seen nationally. After a decade of falling energy prices that followed market liberalisation, since 2006, energy prices in the UK have risen. Graph 1 illustrates this.

Graph 1: Energy prices index between 1990 and 2008

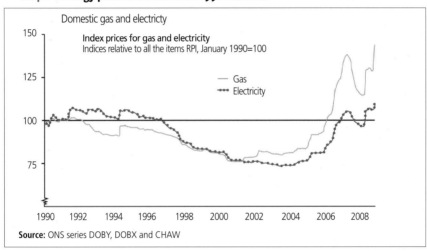

Source: ONS series DOBY, DOBX and CHAW

These price movements have translated into annual expenditure on fuel in the UK almost doubling over the last 10 years.

The consequences of fuel poverty

The most severe consequence of fuel poverty is the excess death rate during the winter months, with the UK's excess death rate being one of the highest in Europe[9] and many of these excess deaths attributed to cold weather.[10] Extreme cold weather can kill through hypothermia, and can worsen respiratory conditions and cardiovascular diseases.[11]

Fuel poverty is also is linked with a range of other social problems such as debt, poorer educational outcomes and social isolation. It is both a cause and a consequence of health and social problems because people with health problems tend to have lower incomes. This means people in fuel poverty can be trapped in a cycle of cold weather creating health problems that lead to reduced incomes, which in turn leads to further exposure to cold.

The consequences of fuel poverty are related to how people cope with cold weather and fuel poverty. The Bevan Foundation's research[12] on coping strategies adopted by people in fuel poverty identified four main behaviours associated with cold weather: (1) disregarding the cost and simply turning the heating up, (2) practical action to stay warm but reducing the cost of doing so, (3) avoidance strategies, and (4) self-disconnection. Each of these strategies has its own consequences.

The first strategy of disregarding the cost of fuel can lead to financial pressures. For people in housing that isn't energy efficient, this behaviour is likely to lead to high fuel bills. This creates the risk that the household will go into debt to be able to afford the cost of energy, or go into arrears. Alternatively, a household in fuel poverty may make other sacrifices to afford a high bill. This could mean going without food and other essentials. Therefore a household in this position can face health problems related to poor diet.

The second strategy of taking practical action is the strategy that is regarded as the sensible 'safe' response. Practical action here can include wearing extra clothing, having a hot drink and adopting sensible financial planning with regard to bills. These kinds of behaviours are not associated with significant health and social problems, unless taken to the extreme. However, for households in fuel poverty, adopting these behaviours alone may not be sufficient to ensure they escape the effects of a cold household or a bill that is unaffordable.

The third strategy involves avoidance strategies and reducing living space. These are behaviours such as only heating one room and staying in that one room, through to going elsewhere (such as a friend/neighbour's house), which have the effect of reducing the living space available to a family. This can then bring problems associated with overcrowded homes such as an increase in family conflict, and lack of privacy. It can affect the education of children as they face the prospect of no privacy with which to pursue school assignments or hobbies. The effects of cold housing also begin to show, as even if one room is adequately heated, others are not and thus may develop mould and deteriorating conditions.

> **Cold houses can cause and exacerbate chronic medical conditions.**

Moving onto the final strategy of self-disconnection, which is essentially the opposite of the strategy of disregarding the cost. Households that adopt this behaviour are those that simply do not use their heating systems and therefore stay cold during winter. The effects of living in a cold house on health have been well documented. Cold houses can cause and exacerbate chronic medical conditions. Cold weather affects the condition of housing, with damp and mould on the walls. The National Public Health Service point out that this has implications for asthma sufferers and those with respiratory conditions,[13] with the recent rise in asthma linked in some circles to mouldy housing. A European study of housing conditions has also found that damp and mould in households can contribute to depression, reinforcing the view that there is a clear link between housing conditions and mental illness.[14]

Fuel poverty can have a disproportionate effect on vulnerable groups such as people with disabilities. For example, people suffering from cancer need to be warm in order to improve their chances of recovery. In a survey of health professionals, MacMillan cancer support found that 85 per cent of health professionals agreed that feeling cold can significantly affect a cancer patient's recovery. The chances of recovery significantly depend on mental well-being, which in turn is affected by external factors such as whether somebody can cope with a significant loss of income. Yet a person diagnosed with cancer is likely to also face a large drop in income. This shows how fuel poverty can reinforce disadvantage – it can cause ill health which can lead to a reduced income, which is then followed by further ill health .

The consequences of fuel poverty in Wales thus largely depend upon how people behave when confronted when cold weather. For some the consequences will be those problems associated with financial difficulties, and for others there will be the consequences of cold homes and reduced living space.

Fuel poverty policy in Wales

The issue of fuel poverty was not identified as a specific public policy issue until the late 1970s, following the oil crises of 1974 and subsequent rise in energy prices. It has only become established as a policy issue alongside concerns about energy efficiency and the environment.[15] During the 1980s the Conservative Government felt that the development and distribution of home insulation was best left to the market, and that the privatisation of energy was trusted as being sufficient to drive down fuel prices. It was only in the 1990s that active government intervention began via the introduction of a grants system to fund home insulation for vulnerable people. There was also the creation of the Energy Saving Trust, and the Home Energy Conversation Act (1995), measures that were firmly designed with one eye on carbon reduction rather than as anti-poverty measures. The Labour Government that was elected in 1997 adopted a more active approach to fuel poverty, aiming to eliminate fuel poverty throughout the UK over the long run. The responsibility for achieving this in Wales was devolved to the newly established National Assembly for Wales.

In 2003 the Welsh Assembly Government published a strategy that aimed to eradicate fuel poverty amongst vulnerable groups by 2010, all residents of social housing by 2012, and entirely in Wales by 2018.[16] The main parts of the strategy have been to provide home insulation and energy efficiency measures to reduce bills, and benefit health checks to ensure the maximum amount of income for households. The main mechanism of delivering these savings has been the Home Energy Efficiency Scheme (HEES), which has supported the installation of energy efficiency measures in over 124,000 homes and also offers benefit health checks to its clients. In addition to this there have been several local initiatives that have been distributing energy efficiency advice and organised bulk buying of energy to reduce costs.

The fuel poverty strategy is linked with wider economic and social goals. Having recognised the potential to create a new industry around the development of energy efficiency products and 'green jobs', the Welsh Assembly Government has launched a major initiative to install 40,000 micro-generation units in homes and thus bring a new industry to the Heads of the Valleys.[17] It has also arranged for a 'green jobs' training centre at Tredegar to provide skills in this developing industry. The fuel poverty strategy has been updated to ensure procurement policies for HEES include clauses so that contractors utilise local labour.

To consider the effectiveness of the fuel poverty strategy we need to recall how people in fuel poverty behave. For those who disregard the cost of fuel and simply turn the heating up, energy efficiency measures are helpful because they will result in lower bills (although not necessarily low enough to lift the household out of fuel poverty). The benefits of this should not be under-estimated, as the savings can be substantial and result in fewer households getting into debt or arrears.

> **energy efficiency measures alone are not the solution to fuel poverty**

However, energy efficiency measures alone are not the solution to fuel poverty. Unless a household is able to afford to heat the home, albeit with a lower bill, the household will remain in fuel poverty whatever the energy efficiency measures. Even when a home is made energy efficient, its occupants still have to find a way to meet their (reduced) bills. Sometimes energy efficiency measures also do not prove as effective in practice in the household as they are in the laboratory. In practice, gains in efficiency are not as great as forecast when they are subjected to the practicalities of every day use.[18] Additionally, the massive savings possible in 'eco-homes' can only be a long-term solution whilst roll-out remains slow.

It is clear then that focus alone on energy efficiency measures will not resolve the problems of fuel poverty. It is increasingly recognised that the Welsh Assembly Government targets for eliminating fuel poverty are going to be missed.[19] This is largely because of substantial price rises in energy from 2006, rises that are likely to continue for the foreseeable future. Despite making homes more energy efficient, energy prices and incomes remain the most important factors in determining the number of households in fuel poverty. Every time prices go up 10 per cent, another 400,000 people enter fuel poverty.[20]

It is this recognition that has led to growing calls for a new approach to tackling fuel poverty. The Institute for Public Policy Research have, alongside energy companies and campaigners, argued for a major rethink of the UK

Fuel Poverty Strategy.[21] They argue that:

A full review would need to reconsider the assumptions that underpin the current strategy and should look at some of the aspects that are taken for granted including the way that fuel poverty is defined, the use of targets to drive forward progress, and the focus on government and energy suppliers as the major delivery agents.[22]

It is clear that such a rethink is necessary, and it is a rethink that needs to account for how people react to cold weather rather than make fuel poverty a technical problem that requires technical adjustments to housing. If the consequences of fuel poverty are largely the result of how people behave when faced with cold weather, then it follows that solutions must account for how people behave. In other words put the poverty back into fuel poverty.

James Radcliffe is policy and research officer at the Bevan Foundation

Notes

1 BBC News (2010) Councils try to keep roads clear despite salt shortage, 9th January. Available from http://news.bbc.co.uk/1/hi/uk/8449755.stm

2 Baker, W. (2001) *Fuel Poverty and ill health – a review*, Centre for Sustainable Energy

3 Welsh Assembly Government (2007) *Fuel Poverty in Wales 2004* Available from http://wales.gov.uk/dsjlg/research/fuelpoverty2004/analysise.pdf?lang=en

4 Gordon, D. and Fahmy, E. (2008) *A fuel poverty indicator for Wales*. University of Bristol/centre for Sustainable energy, available from http://wales.gov.uk/docs/desh/policy/090129fuelpovertyreporten.pdf

5 Consumer Focus Wales (2010) *Domestic Energy Report*, May.

6 Ibid.

7 Welsh Assembly Government (2008) Living in Wales Survey.

8 Department of Energy and Climate Change (2010) *Quarterly Energy Prices*, June available from http://www.decc.gov.uk/assets/decc/statistics/publications/prices/1_20100621134719_e_@@_qe pjun10.pdf

9 Baker, W. (2001) op. cit.

10 Statistics from http://www.healthknowledge.org.uk/parta/paper1knowledge/2_diseasecausationdiagno stic/2f_Environment/2f5.asp

11 Rudge, J. (2007). *The impact of fuel poverty on health: contributing to the evidence base: Non-Technical Summary* (Research Summary). ESRC End of Award Report, RES-000-22-1402.

12 Radcliffe, J. (2010) Fuel Poverty in Wales. The Bevan Foundation: Ebbw Vale

13 Public Health Wales website http://www.wales.nhs.uk/sitesplus/888/page/43768 accessed 9th Nov 2010

14 See http://www.medicalnewstoday.com/articles/80452.php

15 Powells, G. (2009) *Warming homes, cooling the planet, an analysis of socio-techno economic energy efficiency and practice in the UK*, Durham University PHD thesis, 2009

16 Welsh Assembly Government (2003) Warm Homes and Energy Conservation Act: a fuel poverty commitment for Wales. Available from http://wales.gov.uk/about/programmeforgovernment/strategy/publications/housingcommunity/1 239033/?lang=en

17 Welsh Green Generation biggest in UK, news article http://www.newbuilder.co.uk/news/newsFullStory.asp?ID=2774

18 Bell, M. et al (forthcoming) *Findings from Elm Tree Mews*, JRF: York

19 Bird, J., Campbell, R. and Lawton, K. (2010) *The Long Cold Winter: Beating fuel poverty.*
    IPPR: London
20 House of Commons Select Committee on Business and Enterprise (2008) *Energy prices,*
    fuel poverty and Ofgem, Eleventh report of session 2007-8. Available from
    http://www.publications.parliament.uk/pa/cm200708/cmselect/cmberr/293/293i.pdf
21 Bird, J., Campbell, R. and Lawton, K. (2010) op. cit.
22 ibid

The downside
of the **great car economy:**
transport poverty in Wales[1]
Lee Waters

WHEN A HOUSEHOLD SPENDS 10 PER CENT or more of their income on fuel to keep their home warm they are considered to be in 'fuel poverty'. It is a widely understood problem and tackling it is rightly seen as a priority for Government. The concept of transport poverty, however, is little understood.

Transport policy in Wales is centred around the concept of mobility. The Assembly Government regards mobility as "a significant driver of economic growth and social well-being"[2] As a consequence our society is increasingly designed around the assumption that people have access to a car, and it is the role of transport professionals to make it easier for them to travel further and faster.

In the fifteen year period from the mid-80s the distance motorists travelled grew by nearly a third and the number of cars on the road increased by nearly 50 per cent, while journey times remained constant.[3] At the same time use of more sustainable forms of transport fell. To cater for the increasing number of car journeys the Welsh Assembly Government spends more than £300 million a year on building new roads to improve journey times for the transport 'haves'. But it comes at the expense of transport provision for the 'have nots'.

One in four households in Wales is car-less: in Merthyr Tydfil and Blaenau Gwent as many as 36 per cent of homes is without a family car.[4] Yet society is increasingly planned on the assumption that everyone is mobile, and in order to access essential services and jobs low income families often feel it necessary to 'invest' in running a car even when they cannot really afford to do so. Cabinet Office research has found that amongst the poorest fifth of households, those who do own cars spend nearly a quarter of their income on the cost of motoring.[5] Buying and running a car is a major cause of people getting into trouble with debts:[6] Citizens Advice cite cases where being obliged to have a car has led to unmanageable indebtedness. For example:

> A man on a low wage contacted a Citizens Advice Bureau in Cornwall for debt advice. He needed a car in order to get to work, as he lived in a rural area with very poor public transport. But he could only buy one with credit at 42 per cent APR.[7]

This can be a particular problem in rural areas. Research by the Commission for Rural Communities in England found that a lack of accessibility is

> **One in four households in Wales is car-less yet society is increasingly planned on the assumption that everyone is mobile**

making low income households run a car when they might not if they lived in areas with better transport services.[8] Indeed recent work by Gwynedd County Council found widespread transport poverty with over half of households in the county spending more than 10 per cent of their income on fuel costs.[9]

Access denied

The consequence of our unbalanced transport policy has lead not only to further poverty for lower income groups but social exclusion too. "Not having access to a car in a society built around the car is to be disenfranchised in a way that can impact on how you access every other kind of good or service", a report for the Welsh Consumer Council concluded.[10]

A landmark report by the Cabinet Office's Social Exclusion Unit in 2003 found that transport policy had placed key services out of reach of the poorest.[11] For example:

- Two out of five jobseekers say lack of transport is a barrier to getting a job.

- For young people, inaccessibility of work is cited as the most common obstacle to getting employment.

- Nearly half of 16-18 year olds struggle to afford the cost of transport to reach their education.

those on low incomes have faced a 'double-whammy' as the cost of public transport has risen

As services became more difficult to access without a car those on low incomes have faced something of a 'double-whammy' as the cost of public transport has risen. Whilst the last three decades saw the cost of motoring fall by 17 per cent in real terms, the cost of public transport increased over the same period.[12] In Cardiff some single bus fares have risen by up to 186 per cent in just seven years,[13] placing a further barrier in the way of accessing services for those on low incomes.

Passive driving

People who do not use a car are still exposed to the negative impacts of traffic, without getting any of the immediate benefits that are enjoyed by car users. This effect on bystanders, by analogy with tobacco smoking, has been described as 'passive driving'. For example, although they are least likely to own a car, people in the poorest households are more likely to be injured or killed by a car, and this is especially true of children.[14] "There is a clear link between pedestrian accident rates and social class," the Cabinet Office's study concluded. "The evidence is particularly marked for children. Children from social class V are five times more likely to die in a road accident than those from social class I.[15]

The impact of passive driving is particularly clear in health terms. People who live close to busy main roads are more likely to suffer chronic ill-health, as evidenced by symptoms such as runny or blocked nose, sore eyes or sore throat, coughs, or lack of energy, even when other factors such as income are controlled for.[16]

Perhaps the most significant public health impact of rising car use is the increase in sedentary lifestyles. The 2007 analysis by the UK Government's Foresight programme predicted that a majority of UK adults could be clinically obese by 2050, at an annual cost to society of £49.9 billion in today's money.[17] It pointed out that those who are already disadvantaged are more likely to suffer obesity and the considerable problems associated with it.

Being overweight or obese increases the risk of a wide range of chronic diseases, principally type 2 diabetes, hypertension, cardiovascular disease including stroke, as well as cancer. It can also impair a person's well-being, quality of life and ability to earn...Although ...obesity occurs across all population groups, the socially and economically disadvantaged and some ethnic minorities are more vulnerable.

The highest rates of adult obesity are amongst men and women in households in the lowest income quintile, and childhood obesity has also risen fastest amongst children from poorer backgrounds.[18] Obesity arises from multiple factors, including diet and occupation. It is also clearly linked to a fall in levels of physical activity and the declining levels of walking and cycling. People from the poorest households are the most likely to be sedentary and less likely to meet physical activity recommendations – achieving less than 30 minutes of physical activity per week.[19] In the most deprived areas of Wales; people are twice as unlikely to take exercise.[20]

" pavements are often not provided on new roads; barriers are erected where people desire to cross roads

The Foresight report also recognises the key role of what it terms an 'obesogenic environment'. Changes to the physical environment which reduce opportunities to travel actively by walking or cycling in turn encourage sedentary lifestyles. For example road layouts of new developments have tended to be designed as transport corridors for cars and not laid out to encourage people to walk or cycle around their neighbourhood. The car-centric nature of new neighbourhoods is highlighted by the parking standards which house builders are required to abide by. New houses have to be built with between one and three car parking spaces for every dwelling, with an additional visitor space for every five houses. Furthermore pavements are often not provided on new roads; barriers are erected where people desire to cross roads; developments are not permeable for people travelling on foot or by bicycle requiring them to take circuitous routes. These and other factors have contributed to a built environment which serves to discourage active travel and has contributed to a long-term decline in the number of journeys made by foot and bicycle and a rise in the number of journeys made by car.

Bad habits

The cumulative impact of the policy and practices of our car-centric culture has been to entrench our dependency on the private motor car. Research by Rhondda Cynon Taf Council in July 2010 found that a lack of familiarity and confidence in using public transport along with false perceptions of travel alternatives were significant barriers to using sustainable forms of transport. For example the report noted:

"The students' general level of confidence, and their confidence in using transport, also affected their willingness to travel. Students commented on 'safety' being an issue preventing them from utilising public transport.

"Although cycling and walking were recognised as modes of transport, it was highlighted that these forms of transport are amongst the least safe modes of travel available for them, although they recognised that this mode of transport would have significant health benefits, as well as helping to reduce congestion and carbon emissions."[21]

The research echoes the findings of in-depth studies into perceptions of travel behaviour in the Sustainable Travel Towns programme in England. Research conducted across the three towns (Darlington, Peterborough and Worcester) between 2004 and 2008 showed that people are swayed in **their travel choice by severe misperceptions about the alternatives to the car and a lack of information** (especially relating to relative travel times) and a lack of information. For example, on average across the three towns:

- people over-estimated travel time by public transport by around two thirds and for cars under-estimated travel time by one fifth; and
- in around half of all cases where a viable public transport alternative existed for a local journey made by car, people did not know about it.

Overall, the research showed that while 35 per cent of all people's trips within the towns were already made by sustainable means (using existing facilities by walking, cycling and/or public transport), there was potential for a further 29 per cent of trips to be shifted from car to walking, cycling or public transport without any infrastructure changes or restrictions on car use. This conclusion in particular gave the Sustainable Travel Towns confidence that through the coordinated use of 'soft' measures to provide information, motivate or otherwise influence people's daily travel choices, car use could be significantly reduced.

The research concluded that with the right information and some encouragement people could nearly double their use of sustainable modes tomorrow, and in the longer-term targeted investment in infrastructure – such as 20mph zones and safe routes to school, together with more rational land use planning – could enable nine out of ten journeys to be made on foot, by bike or using public transport.[22]

How much?

Whilst the cost of motoring has declined over time, fuel prices have risen significantly in recent years and threaten to challenge the viability of continuing to place the concept of mobility at the centre of transport policy.

When fuel protestors threatened to bring the UK to a standstill in 2000, motorists were paying an average of 80 pence a litre for unleaded and 80.8 pence for diesel.[23] Ten years later unleaded stands at 119 pence and diesel 122 pence. Despite the impact of the recession oil prices remain at a high rate historically. A report by Chatham House and the insurers Lloyds warned prices are likely to rise in the short to mid-term as supplies become more difficult.[24] That analysis was confirmed by an Industry Taskforce on Peak Oil and Energy Security, consisting of leading companies from the power, engineering and transport sectors, which warned that "the era of cheap oil is behind us. We must plan for a world in which oil prices are likely to be both higher and more volatile".[25] UK Energy Secretary Chris Huhne has estimated that if the oil price doubled, it could lead to a cumulative loss of GDP of around £45 billion over 2 years – the equivalent of the entire Ministry of Defence budget in 2008/09.[26]

If oil prices continue to rise over coming years transport injustice already experienced by millions could be suffered by many more

If, as seems likely on the basis of present evidence, oil prices continue to rise over coming years and decades, transport injustice already experienced by millions could be suffered by many more.

Conclusion

Our great car economy leaves large parts of our society in the slow lane. The goal of enabling people to travel further and faster has seen our towns, suburbs and countryside re-shaped to accommodate mass car ownership, all made possible by a ready supply of fuel sold at the pumps for roughly the price of mineral water. As the price of oil rises many more people are likely to find themselves struggling with the cost of car use. If our society continues to be shaped on the assumption that we can all 'hop in the car', the proportion of people experiencing injustice and exclusion will grow.

The steps required to make our transport system socially just are the same steps needed to make the transport system less carbon-intensive and more robust to oil price shocks. It is time to move beyond mobility as the central organising principle of our transport system and instead focus on accessibility for all.

Lee Waters is the National Director for Wales of the sustainable transport charity Sustrans

Notes   1   This chapter draws on *Towards Transport Justice: Transport and Social Justice in an Oil-Scarce Future*, April 2008. Prepared for Sustrans by Ian Taylor and Lynn Sloman.
2   Welsh Assembly Government (2008) *One Wales Connecting the Nation: the Wales Transport Strategy*. WAG: Cardiff. p.6
3   Average trip lengths rose by 29 per cent between 1985/86 and 1999/2001 according to the Department for Transport's National Travel Survey. During this period average journey times increased only marginally (from 20 to 21 minutes) indicating that average journey speeds have increased: over the same time car ownership increased from 16.4 million to 23.9 million, a 45 per cent increase (Department for Transport (2008) Vehicle Statistics).
4   2001 Census data
5   Social Exclusion Unit (2003) *Making the Connections: Final Report on Transport and Social Exclusion*, Cabinet Office: London. p.3
6   For example, necessity to own a car is listed in the top seven causes of problem debt by advice line Breathing Space, at http://www.breathingspacescotland.co.uk/bspace/113.3.28.html, accessed 7/11/2007
7   Transport 2000 Trust, Countryside Agency and Citizens Advice Bureau, (2003) *Rural Transport Futures*, p.3.
8   In the lowest income group [quintile] between 72 per cent and 88 per cent of households in hamlets and villages own a car, compared to between 46 per cent and 53 per cent in towns and urban areas (Commission for Rural Communities (2007) *The State of the Countryside*, p.27.
9   Cyngor Gwynedd Council (2007) *Living in Gwynedd: an examination of the costs and issues arising from living on the periphery*
10   Welsh Consumer Council (2004) *People Without Cars,* WCC: Cardiff
11   Social Exclusion Unit (2003) op. cit.
12   House of Commons, Written Answers for 19 March 2009
13   Western Mail, 20th September 2010
14   Institute for Public Policy Research (2002) *Streets ahead: Safe and liveable streets for children*. IPPR: London
15   Social Exclusion Unit (2003) op. cit. pp.17-18
16   Whitelegg, J., and Gatrell, A., (1995) *The association between health and residential traffic densities*. World Transport Policy and Practice volume 1(3)
17   Government Office for Science Foresight Programme (2007) *Tackling Obesity Future Choices project report*. 2nd edition, p.5
18   Law, C., Power, C., Graham, H., & Merrick, D. (2007) Department of Health Public Health Research Consortium, Obesity and health inequalities, commissioned by the Foresight programme of the Office of Science and Innovation, Department of Trade and Industry, Obesity Reviews 8 (Suppl. 1), p., 19–22
19   For example, 44 per cent of women and 34 per cent of men in the poorest households in England are sedentary, compared to only 33 per cent of women and 28 per cent of men in the wealthiest households. Sustrans Active Travel Information sheet FH12, *Active travel and health inequalities*. November 2008
20   Drakeford, M. (2006) *Health Policy in Wales: Making a difference in conditions of difficulty*, Critical Social Policy, 26
21   'Is transportation a barrier that impacts on the ability of young people to participate in society?' *Report of the transportation scrutiny working group. Rhondda Cynon Taf Environmental Services Scrutiny Committee*, 6th July 2010.
22   Department for Transport (2010) *The Effects of Smarter Choice Programmes in the Sustainable Travel Towns*. DfT: London
23   "Petrol price rise anger". *BBC News*, 7th September 2000. http://news.bbc.co.uk/1/hi/business/913614.stm. Retrieved 7/10/10
24   Froggatt, A. and Lahn, G. (2010) *Sustainable Energy Security: Strategic Risks and Opportunities for Business*. Chatham House – Lloyds 360° Risk Insight White Paper.
25   Conservative Party (2010) *Rebuilding Security – Conservative Energy Policy for and Uncertain World*, March.
26   Huhne, C. (2010) *Green growth: the transition to a sustainable economy*, Speech to LSE, 2 November

Digital
exclusion,
divided Wales[1]

Victoria Winckler and James Radcliffe

BROADBAND INTERNET IS CHANGING the economy and society in ways that were unthought-of a decade ago. From being the province of the few interested in IT, it has become a near necessity for a substantial proportion of the population. Goods and services are increasingly delivered via broadband, including everything from grocery shopping to music and TV programmes to claiming Job Seekers' Allowance and applying for jobs.

However, not everyone has had access to broadband – certain communities and some individuals in Wales, as elsewhere in Britain, have had long-standing difficulty with broadband connection. The plight of these, often rural, communities has attracted much attention over the years, and has been addressed in the recommendations on the Universal Service Commitment recently made in the UK Government's *Digital Britain* report.[2] Considerably less attention has been given to households and individuals who do not take up internet or broadband.

Despite the much publicised 'not-spots', Wales has near universal availability, with 99.98 per cent of households connected to a DSL-enabled local exchange.[3] However, there is another aspect of access to broadband which is arguably more important than infrastructure, namely people's take-up and use of the internet. There is no doubt that the proportion of households who access the internet via broadband has increased dramatically in recent years. The Welsh Assembly Government state that broadband take-up rose from 15 per cent of households in 2004 to 58 per cent in 2008.[4] Personal access to the internet has also increased, with Consumer Focus Wales reporting that 69 per cent of people had access to the internet in 2009, up from 47 per cent in 2006.[5]

Geographical variations

Much of the debate about the 'digital divide' in Wales has focused on geographical variations in broadband take-up, in particular those between rural and urban areas. However, if the question of take-up rather than physical infrastructure is considered, a rather different picture emerges (Table 1).

Consumer Focus Wales (and its predecessor, Welsh Consumer Council) surveys have consistently shown that people living in the south Wales Valleys are less likely to have a household internet connection than those in other parts of Wales. In 2009 60 per cent of households in the South Wales Valleys had an internet connection compared with 76 per cent of those living in Cardiff and south east Wales.[6]

Table 1: Responses to the question 'are you connected to the internet at home?'

Percentage of Households responding yes	2002	2003	2004	2005**	2006	2009
North	28	38	42	51	43	66
Mid West	42	44	41	34	49	63
West South	34	33	42	39	48	67
Cardiff & SE	41	38	41	48	53	76
Valleys	27	34	37	26	40	60
ALL WALES	35	37	41	41	47	67

** 2005 data should be treated with caution.
Source: Welsh Consumer Council, 2004, 2007b; Richards 2009.

Socio-economic variations

> **Take-up of the internet broadly parallels other socio-economic inequalities**

Take-up of the internet broadly parallels other socio-economic inequalities. It is strongly related to income – the higher an individual's income, the more likely he or she is to have used the internet. In 2006, 51 per cent of adults with an income of £10,400 or less had never used the Internet. In contrast, 93 per cent with an income of £36,400 or more had used the Internet in the 3 months prior to interview, more than twice the proportion (43 per cent) of those earning £10,400 or less.[7]

Specific research on children and young people has found that not having access to the internet at home is strongly related to social class.[8] While 97 per cent of children from social class AB have internet access at home, only 69 per cent of children from social class E have this. Other disadvantaged groups include those whose main language is not English and children in lone parent households, who are also less likely to have internet access than others.[9]

There is also evidence to suggest that disabled people use the internet less than non-disabled people. Ofcom's annual consumer experience reports[10] found that in 2008 only 42 per cent, 32 per cent and 36 per cent respectively of people with visual, hearing and mobility impairments had broadband access at home, as opposed to around 60 per cent of the general population, echoing earlier findings.[11]

Adults under 70 who had a degree or equivalent qualification were most likely to have the internet in their home, at 93 per cent in 2008. Those individuals who had no formal qualifications were least likely to have an internet connection in their home, at 56 per cent.[12]

Older people are the least likely to use the internet. In 2008, 70 per cent of adults aged 65 plus stated they had never used it compared with a negligible number of 16 – 24 year olds and just 8 per cent of 25-44 year olds.[13]

The exception to the association between internet use and disadvantage is ethnicity. Overall, people from ethnic minority groups are 'at the forefront of digital device take-up and use', including use of the internet.[14] There are variations between different ethnic groups, however, and by age within ethnic minority groups.

Most survey evidence focuses on internet access from home. However a growing proportion of people use computers and access the internet elsewhere, either using mobile technology or using computers located outside the home. In 2009, 37 per cent of people had used the internet outside of the home. There are 330 libraries in Wales open over 10 hours a week providing more than 2,600 computers for public use.[15]

The Consumer Focus Wales survey in 2009 asked non-internet users why they did not use the internet. The biggest reason was that people just don't want to use it (41 per cent) followed by not knowing how to use the internet (27 per cent). Figure 1 shows the responses in full.

Figure 1: Reasons why people don't use the internet

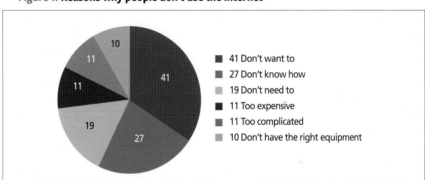

- 41 Don't want to
- 27 Don't know how
- 19 Don't need to
- 11 Too expensive
- 11 Too complicated
- 10 Don't have the right equipment

Other reasons given in other studies for not using the internet are not having a personal computer or worries about spam or viruses.

Does using the internet matter?

Different social groups' use of the internet would not matter if internet use did not bring with it significant social, economic and cultural advantages.

Non-users of the internet face increasing disadvantages. Those not using the internet are unable to access goods and services that are delivered solely digitally, from price comparison services to internet-only offers. They cannot access certain information, be it about health conditions or what is on locally or their bank account balance, nor receive the latest information e.g. news and weather updates. They may also suffer financial penalties as certain goods and services offer on-line discounts e.g. gas and electricity services, or experience delays sending information by post rather than submitting it on-line. Last, but by no means least, people miss out on leisure activities and creative development which it is argued is increasingly part of the "social glue" for friends, families, communities of interest and society as a whole.

The Consumer Research Panel found that it was widely believed that very soon people without broadband would be at a significant disadvantage, as more and more services are offered on-line. They concluded that:

'in the not-too-distant future **not** *having broadband at home is expected to mean reduced options and financial penalties.'*[16]

> **lack of access to and use of the internet does not just reflect social disadvantages, it *reinforces* them**

For these reasons, the Digital Britain report[17] concluded that broadband is:

'an essential facility for citizens and consumers in a modern society', as important as utilities such as gas and electricity. People without broadband will be at a 'significant disadvantage'.

Given that those without broadband are already likely to be disadvantaged e.g. by low income or poor educational qualifications, lack of access to and use of the internet does not just reflect social disadvantages, it *reinforces* them.

Promoting digital inclusion – policy context

As well as action on infrastructure, the UK and Welsh Assembly Governments are actively promoting digital inclusion. The Welsh Assembly Government established Communities @One in 2006 to help people to use technology in the communities that needed it most. The project provided support to community groups and voluntary sector organisations, enabling them to engage with technologies in ways that were relevant to their lives. It included a grant fund to help community and voluntary groups access the technologies that would benefit community members.

A recent evaluation of the programme[18] looked at twelve case-studies, nine examining activity in individual Communities First areas and three based on relatively large-scale projects. Three 'control group' areas were also examined for comparison. The findings of the evaluation were broadly positive: more than 200 projects succeeded in disbursing more than £7 million, without moving away from the original emphasis on supporting small community projects. Many of the projects offered new opportunities in terms of access to ICT and to the skills and confidence to use it too, mainly to individuals who otherwise had little exposure to such technology. The projects were diverse, ranging from drop-in facilities open to the community to more innovative projects working with voluntary and community groups to apply ICT to their core activities; this was also intended to stimulate an interest on the part of individual members with digital technologies as a result.

Communities 2.0 was announced early in 2009 and is following a similar approach to Communities @One, with nearly £20 million over six years being allocated to voluntary and community groups, with increased emphasis on social enterprise and the sustainability of projects.

Improvements in ICT skills in Wales are a fundamental part of the curriculum framework for 3-19 year olds,[19] and the recent Welsh Assembly Government Schools ICT Strategy Group report[20] highlighted some of the issues faced when trying to improve ICT attainment including: (1) the need to address the inequalities in the provision of hardware, connectivity and technical/advisory support for schools across Wales; (2) the need to ensure that learners are not disadvantaged through lack of access to technology beyond school; and (3) the assertion that ICT should be a vehicle for promoting inclusion, not for widening gaps in opportunity and outcomes, recognising that not all learners have access to ICT outside schools and are potentially at a disadvantage because of this.

One of the main portals for teachers and others is the National Grid for Learning Wales (NGfL), which has recently been revamped to reflect more current, collaborative technologies. The Strategy Group report also highlighted the fact that innovation through the use of technologies such as wikis, blogs, open source content management platforms such as Moodle and even mobile technology was becoming more common in many schools, as both teachers and students engage and take more control of their ICT use. It is interesting to note that according to Estyn[21], the use of ICT in primary schools is currently increasing rapidly. Atkins[22] shows clearly that there is a real dividend to be gained from investing in ICT in schools and colleges.

In addition to provision of ICT skills for children and young people, there is also provision for adult learning. Work-based learning through ICT is increasingly part of the delivery of a wide range of skills, including communications, leadership and management, foreign language training, IT (both for technology professionals and those who use IT in their day-to-day jobs), health and safety and other company-specific programmes.[23] However, the extent of use of these programmes is difficult to gauge, and the indications are that although up to 35 per cent of work-based learning providers can be classified as e-enabled, around one quarter of providers are unlikely to be realising the benefits of technology-supported learning.[24] Again recent reports show clearly that there would be further benefit with developing the use of broadband and ICT generally in this area.[25]

Conclusion

As more and more essential services are delivered on-line it is vital that everyone in Wales is able to access the internet and make full use of it. Yet it is clear that although broadband take-up has undoubtedly increased rapidly, access amongst some socio-economic groups – particularly amongst the lowest income households and amongst older people – remains low. Whilst there is geographical variation in take-up within Wales, this seems to reflect patterns of socio-economic disadvantage rather than any geographical factors per se. With take up amongst socio-economic group DE at 40 per cent and that of over-65s at just 26 per cent the issue is one of social exclusion.

The overwhelming reason people give for not accessing the internet is that they do not want to. However as the reasons for this inevitably include lack of awareness, lack of skills and lack of opportunity as well as simple 'choice', it should not be taken at face value, particularly given the massive advantages internet use can bring. It is also worth noting that perceived cost was a factor in lack of access to the internet in a substantial minority of households.

Last, but by no means least, is the question of skills, services and content. The increasing provision of services only via the internet, or the premium paid by users of non-internet services, means that those without access will find it increasingly difficult to obtain certain services, will pay a penalty for goods and services bought off-line, and will be increasingly excluded from the mainstream of society. Very often little consideration is given by those designing internet services to access for those without the internet. Whilst libraries and community centres have a role to play here, the extent of such services is not clear nor is their ability to guide and support novice users.

> **The increasing provision of services only via the internet, or the premium paid by users of non-internet services, means that those without access will find it increasingly difficult to obtain certain services**

The question remains, therefore, whether public policy and action to encourage digital inclusion are sufficient and, if not, what more should be done. The Manifesto for a Networked Nation[26] recommends that the public sector create a series of 'nudges' aimed at encouraging people to go on-line. For example it argues that the Department for Work and Pensions should introduce an expectation that people of working age should apply for benefits on-line and have the skills to look for, and apply for work on-line. There is a risk that 'expectation' will swiftly become an obligation once this proposal travels through the public policy climate at a time of spending cuts and the stigmatization of benefit claimants. The policy may become all stick and no carrot. It is clear that such policies aimed at encouraging people to go on-line may in fact be counter-productive, and end up reinforcing exclusion rather than tackling it.

Use of the internet over the past decade has increased rapidly and is now part of the norm in society. There have been corresponding initiatives aimed at ensuring everyone can enjoy those benefits, but these are risk in the current climate. Unless further support is given to those who do not use the internet, and schemes aimed at bringing people on-line are improved and adequately funded, a technology that promises to be extremely empowering for the citizen may be one that reinforces powerlessness amongst the most vulnerable.

Victoria Winckler is Director and James Radcliffe is Policy Officer at the Bevan Foundation

Notes   1   This chapter is based on a report published by the Bevan Foundation in 2009 titled Digital
          Wales, Divided Wales. It was supported by BT.
         2   Department for Innovation, Business and Skills (2009) *Digital Britain*. Available from
             http://interactive.bis.gov.uk/digitalbritain/report/
         3   Ofcom (2009) *Communications Market Report; Nations and Regions: Wales*
         4   Welsh Assembly Government (2009) Memorandum submitted to the Welsh Affairs Select
             Committee Inquiry into Digital Inclusion in Wales, Available at:
             http://www.publications.parliament.uk/pa/cm200809/cmselect/cmwelaf/memo/diw/ucdiw
             802.htm
         5   Richards, S. (2009) *Locked in or locked out: consumer access to the internet in Wales*,
             Consumer Focus Wales.
         6   Ibid
         7   ONS (2006) *Internet Access 2006: Households and Individuals*. Available at:
             http://www.statistics.gov.uk/pdfdir/inta0806.pdf
         8   BECTA. (2008). *Harnessing Technology Review 2008:The role of technology and its impact
             on education*. Coventry: BECTA.
         9   Peters, M., Seeds, K., Goldstein, A., and Coleman, N. (2007). *Parental Involvement in
             Children's Education, London, DCSF.* London: Department for Children, Schools and
             Families.
        10   Ofcom (2008) *The Consumer Experience 2008 Research Report*. Available at:
             http://www.ofcom.org.uk/research/tce/ce08/research.pdf
        11   Pilling, D., Barrett, P., and Floyd, M. (2004) Does the Internet Open Up Opportunities for
             Disabled People? York: Joseph Rowntree Foundation. Available at:
             http://www.jrf.org.uk/publications/does-internet-open-opportunities-disabled-people
        12   ONS (2008) *Internet Access 2008: Households and Individuals,* Available at:
             http://www.statistics.gov.uk/pdfdir/iahi0808.pdf
        13   Ibid
        14   Ofcom (2008) op. cit.
        15   Richards (2009) op. cit.
        16   Communications Consumer Panel (2009) *Not online, not included:
             consumers say broadband essential for all*. Available at:
             http://www.communicationsconsumerpanel.org.uk/downloads/not%20online%20not%
             20included%20web.pdf
        17   Department for Business, Innovation and Skills (2009) op. cit.
        18   Welsh Assembly Government. (2008) *Evaluation of the Communities@One programme.*
             Cardiff: Welsh Assembly Government.
        19   Welsh Assembly Government. (2008) *Skills framework for 3 to 19 year-olds in Wales.*
             Cardiff: Welsh Assembly Government.
        20   Welsh Assembly Government. (2008) *Transforming Schools with ICT: The report to the
             Wales Assembly Government of the Schools ICT Strategy Group.* Cardiff: Welsh Assembly
             Government.
        21   Estyn. (2007). *Better Schools Fund Provision for ICT in Schools* . Cardiff: HM Government.
        22   Atkins Ltd. (2006) *Benefits of Broadband and the BBW Programme to the Welsh
             Economy.* Newport: Atkins Management Consultants.
        23   Overton, L., Hills, H., and Dixon, G. (2007). *Towards maturity: Looking at the impact of e-
             learning in the workplace.* London: e-Skills UK.
        24   BECTA (2008) op. cit.
        25   Atkins Ltd. (2006) op. cit.
        26   Lane Fox, M. (2010) *Manifesto for a Networked Nation*. Available at:
             http://raceonline2012.org/manifesto

7. CONCLUSION

Headlines and 'small things'
filling in the pictures
of poverty and social exclusion
Gideon Calder

THIS BOOK HAS SET OUT the landscape of poverty and social exclusion in contemporary Wales, and again and again reminds us just how complex that landscape is. The scope of the foregoing chapters is both panoramic and intimate. On the one hand, moving through them, we are confronted by arresting statistics about the general lie of the land. In terms of the distribution of resources, life chances and capabilities it is starkly, stubbornly uneven. From the analyses in part 2 we learn both that Wales has among the highest rates of child poverty in the UK, and that 119,000 older people are estimated to be living in poverty – as meanwhile, working-age poverty is also higher than the UK average. We find in part 3 that there are especially strong links in Wales, by international comparison, between socio-economic disadvantage and educational under-achievement. From part 4 we gain a less-than-reassuring picture of the prospects for improving housing for those in Wales on low incomes. We find in part 5 that health inequalities are widening, and in part 6 the particular contributions that poor access to fuel, online resources, financial services and transport have made to the wider sweep of inequality. For those committed to the aim of reducing such inequalities, the panoramic view is by no means a happy one.

> **For those committed to the aim of reducing such inequalities, the panoramic view is by no means a happy one**

But set against this backdrop, we find another kind of perspective in the rich, pressing insights of individuals living with inequality. These are stories of mundane struggle which the broader panorama of figures, indices and trends cannot by themselves reveal. "Life," as Ida Turley, caring for her husband John, puts it, "is made up of small things." The details she gives of those small things – the everyday loneliness of the carer's role, the frustrations of receiving patchy services, the sense of not being listened to – resonate as strongly as any statistic might. Each of the stories of Amy and Jane and Sian and Margaret and Mark and James and Naomi are told with a similar kind of expertise. It's the kind of wisdom which comes from working with the effects of poverty and social exclusion, rather than just surveying them from a distance. This wisdom is vital. Tackling social exclusion is not just a mathematical exercise, achievable solely through the achievement of more favourable statistics, or the reversal of downward trends. Certainly, policy is essential – and better thinking about policy is a necessary condition for any serious attempt to address inequality. But it is not sufficient. For tackling social exclusion is always, in large part, about paying attention to the shape of individuals' lives. At every stage from the personal story to the analysis of broad socio-economic trends, it is, in the end, the scope for improving those lives which is at stake. It is because this scope is multi-dimensional that there is such value in combining exploration of "headlines" and general trends with due attention to "small things".

So keeping in view the balance between wider structure and individual agents, between macro and micro aspects of poverty and exclusion, is always key. And it is perhaps especially important in the current political climate, where the Conservative/ Liberal Democrat coalition government at Westminster is undertaking a series of heavy cuts in public spending. This spending review comes on the back of a structural analysis of current economic parameters which is as questionable (and rejected, for example, by several recipients of the Nobel Prize for Economics) as it is ideologically essential for Coalition purposes. Of course, the measures are in large part a set of *political* decisions, however much the Westminster government would like us to see them as an "inevitable" response to the budget deficit. The UK debt ratio has been much higher previously – for example, after the Second World War – without governments of whichever party deeming such drastic cuts necessary, and without subsequent events vindicating any such judgement. Dramatising the deficit in the way they have, has allowed the Conservatives, as Ross McKibbin has put it, "to transform a crisis of the banks into a crisis of the welfare state".[1] Which provides, one might say, a convenient opportunity to finish the job of shrinking state welfare provision envisaged, but only partially achieved, by the Thatcher government of the 1980s.

Devolution makes the current political situation different. Cardiff priorities will differ from those at Westminster. As I write, the Welsh Assembly Government is preparing to announce its own budget in response to the Westminster agenda. We know that, for one reason and another, this will shape what it is possible to achieve – in terms of addressing inequalities – in the short and medium term. The implications of this will unfold in due course. Meanwhile, though, we know that social welfare, and in particular the combating of poverty, come under immediate threat when the political climate is as it currently is. This accentuates existing challenges at policy level, and threatens to increase the burdens of those, like Jane Williams ("Jane's Story"), doing their best to get by in conditions of poverty. As the scene changes, and we move beyond the European Year for Combating Poverty and Social Exclusion, various points are important to bear in mind. Each of these is borne out, in varying ways, in the wide array of contributions which make up this book. Each is a complexity which needs to be tackled.

A first, highlighted so effectively throughout this book, is that poverty and social exclusion come in a very wide variety of forms. These are discrete in terms of both their causes and their effects, even though they will overlap in these respects. In turn, combating these different forms presents different kinds of challenge. So the specific nature of transport exclusion, and the particular impacts of the prioritising, as Lee Waters puts it, of "mobility" over "access", stems from distinct economic, sociological and political sources, in important ways unrelated to those connected to child poverty. There is no catch-all solution here; we face trade-offs and difficult decisions if we are to address both symptoms simultaneously. For example, the improvement of access to public transport, through the introduction of better integrated and cheaper services, would have clear social and environmental benefits. But whether there is a common measure to determine whether these benefits would be greater than those stemming from increased investment in housing, or in health, is debatable. If there is such a measure, it would need to be duly complex and nuanced. It is one thing to win the argument in favour of prioritising the tackling of poverty and social exclusion. It is another to get the measure of their many different dimensions, and to coordinate a response to all which does justice to the particularity of each.

A second point is the importance of combining improved distribution of resources with the kinds of cultural shifts which are required for a more equal and inclusive society. Discussing social justice, the political theorist Nancy Fraser draws a helpful distinction between "redistribution" on the one hand, and "recognition" on the other.[2] Redistributive measures concentrate on economic resources: so in the context of combating poverty, on income equality. Recognition, by contrast, concerns social relations. From this point of view, social inclusion requires both a more equal distribution of wealth, and changes in people's perceptions of each other, and their experience of treatment by the state. The importance of both resounds throughout the personal contributions to this volume. People need financial support; they also need to feel respected. There are currently drastic inequalities between the resource-rich and the resource-poor, and the recognition-rich and the recognition-poor. A thriving civil society requires attention to both aspects.

A third point concerns the relation between poverty and social exclusion themselves. Talk of "social exclusion" has become increasingly widespread since the early 1990s, partly because of its enthusiastic take-up by think tanks and governments (such as the post-1997 Labour administration at Westminster). The potential advantages of "social exclusion" are helpfully presented by Hartley Dean:

> [Social exclusion] encompasses the idea that there are many factors – to do with income, resources and lifestyles, access to goods and services, participation in employment and civic life, engagement with friends and relatives – that all bear upon the extent to which people are "included" in society. It is a concept that may be used to describe the dynamics of the processes by which people, at particular points in their lives and for particular reasons, may become distanced or removed from mainstream social activities. It can capture the complexity of the processes by which, for some individuals or social groups, multiple causes of exclusion may intersect and have catastrophic consequences.[3]

These processes are, of course, at the heart of this book. But whether, or to what extent, they are something distinct from poverty itself is debatable. Ruth Lister suggests – rightly, in my view – that social exclusion is best seen as "a way of looking at the concept of poverty, rather than an alternative to it".[4] Thus rather than treating the two as different categories, or as seeing social exclusion as displacing the notion of poverty altogether, it is most accurate and productive to see attention to social exclusion as inherent in any adequate account of poverty itself. Poverty is relational: it concerns the relations between different members of society. Social exclusion is a particularly helpful way of calibrating those relations, and figuring out their implications. But it is not some new development. Arguably, the aim of combating poverty has always, by definition, been about combating social exclusion.

And this intertwining of distinct but inevitably connected trends, phenomena and experiences is something we are pointed towards time and again throughout this book. It will, I hope, be regarded as a valuable resource for practitioners in different fields of social welfare, for political actors and campaigners, and for those, like Jane and Ida, whose life experiences bring the book's themes into the sharpest, most urgent focus.

> **this intertwining of distinct but inevitably connected trends, phenomena and experiences is something we are pointed towards time and again throughout this book**

Gideon Calder is Director of the Social Ethics Research Group at the University of Wales, Newport.

Notes
1   T McKibbin, R. (2010) "Nothing to do with the economy", *London Review of Books*, vol. 32, no. 22, 18 November.
2   See e.g. Fraser, N. (2008) *Adding Insult to Injury: Nancy Fraser Debates her Critics*. London: Verso.
3   Dean, H. (2006) Social Policy. Cambridge: Polity Press, p. 91.
4   Lister, R. (2004) Poverty. Cambridge: Polity Press, p. 74.

Annex CONFERENCE
Report

Conference
Report

Victoria Winckler

ON 23RD SEPTEMBER 2010 more than 80 delegates, from all walks of life, gathered in the YMCA conference centre, Newport to debate poverty and social exclusion in Wales. The event was one the 'regional activities' being held in Wales as part of the European Year 2010 Combating Poverty and Social Exclusion.

The Bevan Foundation is grateful to all the speakers, panellists, chairpersons, delegates, and staff and students of Merthyr Tydfil College for contributing their time and thoughts so freely, making a very successful day.

Morning Session

Keynote speakers

Our conference began with two keynote speakers.

Huw Lewis, the Deputy Minister for Children, gave the opening address. His speech – printed at chapter 2 of this book – left everyone in no doubt of his determination to eradicate poverty, and especially child poverty, even in the tough economic and financial climate ahead.

Peter Kenway, Director of the New Policy Institute, then gave a tour de force overview of poverty in Wales today (a version of which is at chapter 3 of this book). The difficulty of making progress to date and the scale of the challenge ahead provoked a lively debate between Peter, Huw and delegates.

Workshops

Delegates then reconvened in one of five workshops looking at different aspects of poverty. The format of the workshops consisted of a panel of two or three representatives of organisations that provide services to people on low incomes or who are socially excluded who, under the firm guidance of a chairperson, would listen to and respond to comments and questions from service users. Each workshop chair then drew some over-arching conclusions from the discussion.

Education and Learning
Panel: Pam Boyd (ContinYou Cymru) and Jo-Anne Daniels (Welsh Assembly Government)
Chair: Sean O'Neill (Children in Wales)

The starting point of discussion was that every child should have the right to access a quality and inclusive education.

Education and learning were seen to have a crucial role in breaking the cycle of poverty and disadvantage, not just for children but adults too.

"

We need joined-up thinking and joined-up doing

However, the difference in outcomes between children from low income and high income families is substantial. The gap is evident even when children start school, and gets worse as they progress through their education, not helped by, for example, higher rates of 'non-participation' amongst children from low income households. Differences in children's achievement are usually measured by eligibility for Free School Meals, although eligibility is not the same as child poverty.

The workshop also noted the differences in achievement between boys – especially white British boys – and girls; between those in the Heads of the Valleys (Merthyr Tydfil and Blaenau Gwent) and the rest of Wales; and between looked after and other children.

Pam Boyd (left) in the education workshop

The result is that hundreds of children leave school every year at 16 with few or no qualifications.

Delegates then discussed how can we break the cycle through education? What is the role of schools, parents, local authorities and governments?

The Welsh Assembly Government and 'local champions' need to ensure schools are doing all they can to tackle child poverty – some schools do more than others.

Schools need the tools to enable them to overcome child poverty, such as the End Child Poverty Network guide 'Tackling Child Poverty in Schools.' Schools need to understand that they have a role in supporting low income families – especially when schools do not have many pupils eligible for Free School Meals as those who are may feel stigmatized and isolated.

> **The curriculum needs to be able to reflect the community and their needs.**

On the question of early years education, a lot is already being done for example with the Flying Start programme, integrated children's centres, Communities First etc. There is scope for more to be done to support parents and community learning.

How can we improve access to education and lifelong learning? Community-focused schools can re-engage parents, however schools are not always the best environment for parents who had a poor experience of school. Parents' forums, quiz nights and evening activities to attract parents to the school can all help. Community and voluntary sector facilities can help to overcome reluctance to attend school premises. The cost of attending education classes for adults is prohibitive as is the cost of getting to venues, especially in rural communities. E-learning and distance learning have potential here, especially in rural areas, although access to broadband is also an issue.

How can we increase academic achievement? The answer lies in good schools and good teacher role models, who can make the learning experience and school environment more enjoyable. Children need to find school exciting, attractive and safe. Schools need to be more creative to help make sure pupils do not drop out early and disengage. Outside school there is scope to support learning through sport and leisure, Prince's Trust Volunteers, Duke of Edinburgh award schemes etc. Perhaps links should be made with sports providers.

The group then discussed how to ensure that financial barriers to education are removed? The Welsh Assembly Government need to urgently address the additional costs – from school uniforms, to school trips and school meals.

How can we help to prevent children leaving school early? Various ideas were discussed such as partnerships with the voluntary and community sector, vocational training opportunities, and making school enjoyable. The Learning Pathways approach was thought to have potential for under 14s as well as older children.

Housing
Panel: Sioned Hughes (Community Housing Cymru)
and Peter Cahill (Newport City Homes)
Chair: John Drysdale (Tpas Cymru)

The theme of cuts dominated this seminar. Shelter Cymru spoke of a united campaign across the UK against the cuts to housing benefit (HB), one that was focusing on the likely increase in homelessness that would result from this campaign.

There was then some discussion of the effects of changes to HB, particularly the cap on benefit that could be claimed: one person pointed out that when HB rose recently, landlords put rent up to cover the rise in HB. There was concern expressed that landlords are unlikely to reduce the rent when HB is reduced. There was also the concern that as HB is reduced many recipients of it will be forced into housing in multiple occupation (HMOs) and poor quality housing. There was a debate about how badly Wales would be affected compared with London, which was the real target of HB reform.

Housing is the platform for social and health welfare

One delegate explained that HB regulations are a labyrinth. She suggested that any campaign against the cuts needs to have detailed knowledge of what HB is, a detailed knowledge of the likely effects of reform, and to tackle each point made by the government in detail. Above all the campaign needs to show how HB is not a work dis-incentive, and should offer alternative reforms to HB that increase work incentives whilst not leading to homelessness.

A crucial point was then made by the chair, who pointed out that housing is the platform for social and health welfare. If we can put the benefits of good housing at the forefront by explaining how housing can have positive impacts elsewhere in the budget then the prospects for success are better.

There was the discussion of effects of the financial services industry on housing. It was pointed out that an increase in re-possessions may bring

John Drysdale in the housing workshop

house prices down, and subsequently increase the risk associated with housing-related financial products, which was one of the causes of the financial crises.

This led to a discussion of ownership and tenure, with some arguing for a flexible tenure system, but also looking at changing the way we define home ownership. It was emphasised that social housing is people's homes, not a special place where you go when you are poor until you become no longer poor. There is a danger housing is looked at as a temporary thing for poor people, rather than a wider asset that could contribute to society.

The discussion then moved on to consider the scandal of empty homes at the same time as people were homeless. It concluded that whilst the outlook was bleak, there was also an opportunity to think differently about housing and an opportunity for the third sector to step up and offer alternatives.

Health
Panel: Richard Lewis (BMA) and David Jenkins (Chair, Aneurin Bevan Health Board)
Chair: Pam Luckock (NHS Centre for Equality and Human Rights)

This was a wide ranging and lively workshop, with the following issues highlighted in discussion.

The session kicked off on the question of complaints, with delegates asking how service providers could ensure that the process was transparent and effective. The panellists replied that organisations were trying to improve how they handled complaints. Complaints are an opportunity for learning and that in Aneurin Bevan Health Board, for example, there is a board champion for complaints.

we hear about efficiency but to most of us in all honesty it just means cuts

Inevitably there were questions about service change and NHS restructuring. Panellists felt unable to respond to comments about restructuring in North Wales but emphasised that the challenge was how to provide clinically safe services close to where people live. All boards had plans to do as much as possible locally, recognising that more specialized services need to be safe. Decisions like this were sometimes opportunistic but full consultation was vital.

Delegates questioned the withdrawal of free swimming for over 55's and pointed out the impact on health benefits – how is this joined up, they asked?

A discussion about the links between health and social status followed, with health boards being urged to work with other sectors to ensure that services are joined up: health, social care and housing and employment all need to be linked together. The panellists felt that statutory services had to be protected against cuts first, and that safety of services had to be paramount. The challenge was to provide the best services efficiently and with proper consultation.

Richard Lewis commented that doctors in general support moving services from hospital to community, but are concerned that community services are insufficiently developed at present. This will have a bigger impact on the most vulnerable. The challenge is for health boards to get services into the community before moving patients from secondary care. We don't use self help and voluntary sector enough, he suggested.

Delegates then raised a number of varied issues about provision of services. One felt that Black and Minority Ethnic groups, refugees and homeless people are often still excluded in health strategies, and that often there is a lack of information in accessible formats and translation services needed. Some BME communities have specific health needs and communication needs. Another asked how will you ensure that the Human Rights of people with disabilities, especially children with Learning Disabilities, are upheld and ensure that they are not disenfranchised? Have the number of health checks for disabled people increased?

Various points were made about different services including the value of multi-sensory holistic therapies and ICare.

The panellists responded that resources were a challenge – they'd like more money but are not going to get it. There was an opportunity to do things more efficiently, with engagement with Communities and third sector being critical, self-advocacy was important too.

> **"an important aspect of changing service delivery has to be proper consultation ... with the public and health professionals'**

Delegates in the health workshop

Employment

Panel: Roger Dinham (JobCentre Plus) and Deri Ap Hywel
(WorkingLinks)
Chair: Sian Wiblin (President, Wales TUC)

The panellists and audience engaged in an informative and at times critical
debate surrounding employment and social exclusion.

The workshop queried the UK Government's review of welfare provision
arguing that it was not a 'lifestyle choice' to be reliant on benefits. Barriers
to gaining paid employment, particularly in respect of people with
disabilities, were described, with a lack of understanding during
both the benefits and employment process of the requirements of
individuals being identified.

Ongoing in-work support for the individual as well as greater
employer awareness regarding assistance in providing workplace
adjustments was needed.

It was agreed that forging local relationships and collaborative
working between parties engaged in the work placement process
was desirable.

Concern was expressed that there was much to put right at
present, and it was felt that cuts to public sector budgets would
exacerbate current concerns.

> **we're very
> concerned that
> people have a
> literacy problem
> but are told to go
> to that terminal
> over there [to
> find a job]. Job
> applications are
> on the internet
> but perhaps they
> don't have the
> internet at home.
> It takes a long
> time to help
> people with
> literacy problems
> to apply**

*Delegates in the
employment workshop*

Debt and Financial Inclusion
Panel: Kieron Dineen (Newport Credit Union),
Ian Ross (Rathbone Cymru) and Kathy Brown (Barclays)
Chair: Fran Targett (Citizens Advice Bureau)

The workshop was introduced with some statistics about debt and financial inclusion from Citizens Advice Cymru. Bureaux in Wales had dealt with 132,015 debt issues last year, 38 per cent of all enquiries, and a 16 per cent increase on the previous year. Debt related to credit cards and unsecured personal debts remained the largest proportion of these issues but rent debt to housing associations had increased by 35 per cent, to private bailiffs by 78 per cent and fuel debt issues had increased by 28 per cent. Debt intervention was at least £202 million. In addition work on financial capability had increased.

> **people with poor credit ratings need access to small loans**

It was agreed that financial exclusion covered the inability, difficulty or reluctance to access appropriate financial services including money and debt advice, financial capability, banking, affordable credit and insurance, and that the reduction of financial exclusion is a priority as it has direct impact on poverty.

The workshop panel gave short introductions. Ian Ross described how 29 per cent of young people don't know how to manage money, increasing debts among young people and the fact that they don't know where to turn for advice. Kathy Brown explained Barclays' involvement in funding the delivery of financial capability work including Barclays Moneyskills aimed at vulnerable 16-25 year old young people. She talked about the aim of financial capability being to increase people's income, help them avoid debt and enable them to understand how to access affordable credit. Kieron Dineen gave information about credit union saving and borrowing, explained how credit unions could give access to

Fran Targett (centre) with Ian Ross and Kathy Brown in the debt and financial inclusion workshop

cheap loans for their members and made comparisons with the 'doorstep lending' part of the credit industry to illustrate how beneficial encouraging credit union membership was for more vulnerable people.

Key messages from delegates and responses from delegates and panel were:

- Credit unions are better than doorstep lenders but they need to improve their methods of reaching people and especially marketing on a personal basis. There are proposals to do this through better links to community organisations including Communities First and Women's Institutes.

- We need to be clearer about financial credibility and safety of savings – it was agreed there is a need to improve education and awareness of the way credit union savings are underwritten.

- People with poor credit ratings need access to small loans. Moneyline Cymru are able to give small loans and are able to loan under higher risk, though at higher cost, than Credit Unions. This a real alternative to the higher interest charged by the door-step lenders.

- The accessibility of basic bank accounts needs to be improved, including ensuring that commercial banks do not turn away people unnecessarily because of difficulties with producing ID. It was noted that improvements had been made but that there was more to do by the banking sector.

- Concerns were raised about pensioner poverty and the need for both responsible lending and access to credit for older people.

Afternoon Session

The afternoon session focused on 'what works' when tackling poverty and social exclusion.

Two Sisters – a film

The afternoon opened with the premier of a film produced by students and staff at Merthyr Tydfil college, introduced by Gemma Griffiths, who was part of the team which made the film and is its presenter. Gemma narrates the challenges she faces as a university student and part-time worker in a fast-food restaurant, especially now that she has just moved into her own flat:

> "At the moment, I am poor. I've got hardly any money at all. I work in McDonalds. It's not very good pay but [I] coped when I was living with my parents, because all I had to think about is paying my share of the rent, which was £60. But now, I've got to think about bus fare, train fare, rent, gas, electric, water, TV licence, phone bills. Oh, there's just so many bills to pay, you know. I'm just like worried I won't be able to afford it. That's the main worry as well, when you move in."

She talked about her childhood, growing up with her family in Merthyr Tydfil:

> "The majority of all our problems started because Dad was asthmatic. Well, he was asthmatic but it didn't stop him from working until he worked in [a local factory] and it started affecting his chest, because of … all the dust. …"

As the family lived on disability benefits, money was short:

> "Me and my sister would write Christmas lists and we'd never get half of the stuff on our Christmas lists because my parents just couldn't afford to buy us like really big stuff. Almost all of our things are shared. So our TV was shared, our bed was shared, our bedroom was shared."

Looking ahead, she describes how she wants her situation to change:

> "I've got hardly any money at all, so I want to get out of that, so that I can afford the nice things like other people can have. Like, I'm learning to drive at the moment so I want a nice car. I want to be able to have my own house. I want to be a homeowner, so I'd like a big, a nice house you know. I want all that stuff. I want to have enough money to fall back on. I want to have savings, but at the moment I have, I have barely enough money to live on, like now, never mind to put money away to save, so I'd like, I want to get out of it."

The film had a powerful impact on the delegates and has since been extremely well received by many others too. Clips have been screened on and Gemma has been interviewed by Sky News; it has been a feature on BBC Good Morning Wales (10th November 2010) and is on the BBC Wales website, and is to be screened on the Community Channel. It has also received press coverage in the South Wales Echo and Merthyr Express.

Two Sisters, produced by students and staff at Merthyr Tydfil College.

Available at http://www.youtube.com/user/enginehouseprod

Knowledge Café

Delegates then discussed in small groups what action they would like Governments and others to take to tackle poverty and social exclusion. The aim was to compile 'messages for government' that would highlight the issues that delegates felt were most important.

Messages to governments

Approaches

Remove barriers to doing things for yourself – there are some who can and want to help themselves.

People living in poverty should be considered and consulted when developing policies.

Encourage and support innovation – the old ways don't work anymore.

The Welsh Assembly Government should maintain pressure on the UK government to recognise the higher level of poverty in Wales, and create solutions to fit the problems.

Work and worklessness

Support the living wage – make work attractive and encourage quality jobs.

Benefits system should complement the labour market and help people get back into work.

Build on existing alliances to develop credible alternatives to 21st century welfare reforms.

Education and learning

Well funded education recognising effect of vulnerability.

We need to educate our young people for life, thinking of education as a form of personal development.

Attitudes and stereotypes

Eradicate prejudice about poverty in the media, employers, middle classes etc.

Educate the rich about the realities of poverty.

During the discussion, the student film makers interviewed delegates about their views on poverty and social exclusion – they had a lot to say!

"The people who know what's wrong, the ones right at the sharp end who are living it everyday, are not being listened to."

"We need to make people in our own society aware of what poverty exists and what it means, because people don't know."

"'We may be living in poverty but we still have a life."

"Communities can do things for themselves but the power to do this is being taken away."

"The political system is geared against listening to 'that' [people in poverty] voice – The more it's talked about the better."

Beverley Humphreys in coversation with...

In the last session, broadcaster and singer Beverley Humphreys held an open conversation with two people who worked, in different ways, to overcome poverty and social exclusion.

MARK ATKINSON gave an account of his life, from being homeless, living in a tent on a beach in north Wales and using drugs, to becoming NIACE Dysgu Cymru 'adult learner of the year' in 2009.

> *"My lowest point was living in a tent from January to May. … I always wanted to go to university but never felt that I had the opportunity, I never felt encouraged."*

> *"Even the most seemingly down at heel, drug addicted, alcoholic person, even the most outcast of people has potential. … It took a lot of hard work and ingenuity to maintain a 25 year drug addiction. If that ingenuity can be harnessed in a positive way then there is nothing you can't do.'*

There was silence as the audience realised the scale of his struggle against so many challenges, and deep respect for his achievements so far. His reading of his poem drew an inspiring and moving session to a close.

DILYS PRICE described her work with the Touch Trust, a therapy centre for people with severe learning disabilities. Her ambition and determination to overcome any difficulty in her path, including sky-diving more than one thousand times by the age of 78, was remarkable. Her dedication to transforming the lives of disabled people though beautiful experiences was an uplifting end to an extraordinary session.

Delegates at the Knowledge Café

"We've got to go on dreaming the impossible and kicking down doors and fighting and being stubborn in what we believe in"
"We will change the world"
"We all have the right to a fulfilling and fulfilled life"

Beverley Humphreys drew the 'conversation' and the conference to a close. She said she had been 'humbled by the realities of poverty' and reminded us:

"There is a danger to think only of statistics and general titles. Politicians especially talk about 'the homeless', 'the disabled' and 'the poor' but as we know we are talking about real human beings and their stories. Those stories are often the most potent catalyst for opening people's minds and hearts."